WORLD MEMORY
TOURNAMENT
FEDERATION
MANUAL

By Dave Farrow, Chester Santos
Forward by Sergio Gonzales

Copyright © 2013 World Memory Tournament Federation™
Contributions by Dave Farrow, Chester Santos
Forward by Sergio Gonzales
All rights reserved.
ISBN: 1490970185
ISBN-13:9781490970189

Dedication

To: Roland "Rolly" Muller,
1942 – 2013

A Renaissance man in the truest sense.

One of the many great teachers in this world who gave to his students, beyond expectations, comfort, or rewards. Every generation that improves the world started with a teacher like him to guide them.

Contents

Foreword	i
Introduction	1
1. What Are Memory Techniques?	5
2. How Do I Triple My Memory Right Now?	15
3. Sport Memory and Practical Memory	39
4. What is the Journey Method?	49
5. How Do I Memorize Numbers?	61
6. How To Memorize a Deck of Cards	69
7. How Do I Start a Memory Club?	109
8. Memory Tournament Rules	121
9. Tournament Security and Structure	135

"Democratizing Practical Memory"

Foreword by Sergio Gonzales

In three little words lies the potential to profoundly change the way we approach a lifetime of learning. Imagine learning something—anything—empowered by the certainty that memory retention and recall was no longer a limitation, that it was no longer a factor in the equation.

Learn the 1000 most frequently used words in Italian over a weekend. Remember every new, important business contact you just made at a conference. Pick up a guitar and memorize chords and progressions in a shockingly brief amount of time. Know every one of your top 200 customers, their preferences and recent purchases. Recall every muscle, bone and metabolic pathway as a medical student. Perfectly. Every time.

This is the purpose of the **World Memory Tournament Federation**: to democratize practical memory and empower lifelong learning.

One of the things that makes Memory Tournaments so accessible is that the barrier to entry is essentially zero. Our community is founded on a culture of being inclusive and never exclusive. We celebrate individual achievement and at the same time grow together, uplifting the entire community. Diversity enriches our community, providing a vibrant ecosystem that further propels our members with ever-increasing opportunities to grow.

We are open to all skill levels from beginner to Memory Master. Anyone can join our community with absolutely zero experience and in mere minutes see immediate gains in proficiency and experience a sense of achievement. It is this personal journey of attaining mastery that builds confidence and fuels the drive to improve further. There is something special and deeply fulfilling when you watch someone experience memory techniques for the first time, when you see the glint in their eyes and the widening smile that slowly appears as they realize they are doing something within minutes that people have spent a lifetime convincing us is impossible.

We built Memory Tournaments so that any participant can compete on equal footing, regardless of his situation. Learning and success is not limited by funding, access to resources, language or location. A child in a grade school in South Africa can best a graduate with an Ivy League education. Two kids on a playground with a pencil and piece of paper can compete with players who train on the latest tablet devices. The power of the mind and the desire to maximize one's potential is what makes our community special. This is the great equalizer. Our members excel based purely on merit, with unequivocal fairness, bound only by the investment they make in themselves.

Our community comes together around Memory Clubs. A Memory Club is simply a collection of people who have a desire to learn and improve their memory. It is a way for people to connect, to join others in a common endeavour, to support each other and grow together. There is no restrictive definition to what a Memory Club should be, how it should be organized or how it should be run. That is up to its members. It costs nothing to start a Memory Club and nothing to keep it running. All that is needed is the desire to learn. Two people constitute a Memory Club as much as a Memory Club whose members number in the hundreds and thousands. They can meet in person or practice online with members on the other side of the world. All that is needed is two committed individuals. In them resides the power to effect change.

We invite you to join our community, the **World Memory Tournament Federation**™ to experience for yourself what happens when you unlock your potential. Join a Memory Club or start one of your own. Share in the joy of a lifetime of learning and of achieving things previously thought out of reach. Join us as we incite a memory movement.

Introduction

Hi, I'm Dave Farrow, the Two Time Guinness World Record Holder for Greatest Memory and today's Most Requested guest expert on Brain training in the media...

But I didn't always have a good memory. In fact, in high school I had ADHD and Dyslexia and some of the worst grades you've ever seen. I became obsessed with memory and brain training to solve my bad memory. This led to the very first Memory Club in my hometown high school and the best selling memory program in the world.

Now 20 years later you can benefit from my struggle.

In this book, you will discover how to start and run a memory club in your area and help kids avoid the difficulty I had. Who knows, you might help the next great scientist or inventor get better grades!

It all started in 1991, when I started the world's very first memory training club in Kitchener, Ontario, Canada and as far as we know the world's first memory competition. I was only 16, but news of this club appeared in the media worldwide because we could do things like memorize decks of playing cards and rows of numbers, among other incredible feats of memory. But it wasn't just me that could memorize things - it was every other club member too.

Later, in 1995, I became the youngest person to speak in front of a special government commission on education, in an effort to get my early brain-based learning method in schools, so it could help other students.

Back then, the system was very basic. I first learned memory training from such greats as Harry Lorayne, the world famous mentalist. I then went further and created new methods to apply memory training to the real world and overcome things like ADHD, exam studying, business memory and learning issues.

Other contributors to this book took different routes - like Chester Santos, who used this skill to win the U.S. Memory Competition.

While Chester and others were making memory into a game, I was adding to the art of memory by inventing several new techniques. These new techniques made memory training more practical for use in the real world. I wanted to make memory training accessible to real people, not just experts like me. So I developed a new theory, based in neuroscience, called Memory Modes, which explains why memory techniques work in the brain and how they fail, if not taught properly.

Over the years my memory system has become the best selling system of its kind in the world today as well as being featured on over 2000 interviews in the media. It is used by fortune 500 companies, doctors, lawyers and professionals, but also regular individuals who just want to get an edge in life.

But over the years we've just never made any progress in schools.

Until now….

Memory Clubs are coming back!

This book is the definitive guide for Memory Clubs and Memory Tournaments worldwide. There are new ways to compete, get recognition and win prizes, using memory techniques.

Together, with partners from countries all around the world, memory clubs and memory tournaments are sure to take the world by storm.

You are now a part of the

WORLD MEMORY TOURNAMENT FEDERATION

In this book you will learn everything you need to know to start your own memory club, train memory masters, raise money for your club and charities, and achieve amazing feats like memorizing playing cards, 1000 digit numbers and more!

You will discover that memory is not a talent but a skill that can be learned and trained. This skill will unlock hidden talent inside your brain and everyone in your club. Your memory will achieve things you never thought possible in the past.

Our goal is that these clubs will develop the next generation of brain power to help students get better grades and help everyone else gain success in life.

You will be amazed by what you can do!

Chapter 1

What Are Memory Techniques?

Jack Smart - Story by Dave Farrow

Jack Smart sat quietly in his home room class as the teacher handed out a flier for every student to take home. The flier would tell parents about an event happening at the school a month from now.

The bell rang. The noise seemed a million miles away while Jack sat lost in his own world.

"Jack, Smart!" The teacher exclaimed as he turned around to face her.

"If you're done daydreaming could you take a flier from the stack and pass the rest back?"

Jack looked down at the stack of papers that seemed to just appear on his desk. His cheeks went flush red with embarrassment as the class laughed.

His distraction was natural and not truly his fault but it still made him the object of ridicule. He was labeled ADHD. Many people had given up trying to help him succeed.

He was thinking of how his heart sank when he read his midterm report card.

"Student shows no improvement."

He was also diagnosed with Dyslexia a year ago and since that time it seemed to be getting worse. It was a real problem. He would sit down to study and lose concentration in minutes. He would need music or TV on in the background just to pay attention for a few minutes. His mind would wander when it was too quiet. Sometimes when he turned on the TV or radio to fill the silence, he would get hooked. He was engrossed in the program after only a few minutes. An hour would go by and he would still be focused. This is what they called Hyper-Focus, but Jack just called it annoying.

When he was able to force himself to focus, the letters reversed themselves as he read and typed. It frustrated him.

He fell behind.

Jack was distracted by the silence and the worries that filled his head. What would the future hold for someone who can't get his brain to work right?

"You Don't Know Jack"

Parent Teacher Meeting One Week Earlier:

His name was Jack Smart. Smart was literally his name and he was told he had an above average intelligence but he just couldn't make his brain work. He couldn't focus, study or memorize.
There had been talk about holding him back a year just to "catch up" on work. The irony was that school also bored him so holding him back might make things worse.

Jack sat in the guidance counsellor's office after school. He sat with his parents and his counsellor. They talked about him in the third person. Mrs. Bradey, his guidance counsellor, was talking to his parents.
 Talking about 'options' she called them. They talked as if he wasn't in the room.

Jack's mind wandered. He imagined he was a lab rat listening to the doctors plan their next experiment: do we use drugs or run him through more mazes? He imagined aliens with lab coats poking his brain.

"Well Mr. and Mrs. Smart, basically, once a student like Jack falls behind, he rarely recovers. We can try summer school and tutoring but you should consider lowering your expectations." The counsellor said.

Lower your expectations.

That sentence felt like a knife to the heart and pulled Jack out of his day dream.

As Jack sat there listening to adults talk about his future prospects, the kind of job he can hope to get, the type of school he could qualify for, the average income or government assistance for people 'like him', he couldn't shake the bad feeling that this was hopeless! If the experts thought he couldn't catch up, then why try anymore? What was the point of putting out the effort if there was no hope?

Jack's parents sat opposite him and the counsellor. They just listened as the counsellor described his diagnosis and the multiple ways he was failing to achieve success in school. For the first time in his memory, Jack was glad he had the ability to zone out.

Then Jack did a thought experiment: what if the other kids they were talking about - the bad students - sat in the same chair listening to the same conversation?

They would just give up. At least most of them would, he guessed. He visualized them sitting in the same chair. He imagined kids from every background and location. He imagined every race and accent sitting in the same chair simultaneously. Ironically, only a small percentage of people in the world could visualize like this. It was a kind of genius, and he was using this talent to comprehend the scope of his mental faults.

He imagined all these kids diagnosed with learning problems and told they are falling behind. Then he imagined them being told that everyone else in their situation falls farther behind, and never catches up. All the faces in his mind had the same reaction. As he flipped through them in his mind he saw them all simultaneously... give up.

If Jack gave up and stopped trying to solve his learning problems, then he would fall behind even more, just like the kids in his thought experiment.

So when the guidance counsellor said that most students like him fall behind and never catch up, he wondered if it was their fault or if it was because most people just give up when they are told there is not hope?

Jack realized that the label he was given and the words he was told wasn't a prediction, but it was an invitation to give up. It was a real problem. He had focus and memory problems. But more than that, telling a young kid that he has a problem like this does not inspire him to fight, it encourages him to give up. If he gave up, his diagnosis would become a self-fulfilling prophecy and the same counsellor would tell the next kid to give up too.

How could he study and work hard without hope?

He couldn't give up.

Jack suspected part of what he was being told was a lie. Maybe there are no bad students, just unmotivated ones. Then he rejected that thought. It didn't explain his situation. He was trying. Really trying. He would spend hours studying with little results. He was motivated but not able to get his brain to work with him. When he did commit information to memory, once he was tested, the stress would cause him to blank out.

He wished his brain had a manual. Little did Jack know, his wish would soon come true and it would change everything.

"Jack, are you paying attention?" Mrs. Bradey said snapping her fingers. Jack tried to hide his anger at how he was snapped at like a pet. Why would he want to pay attention to people as they called him stupid?

"We are going to assign you a tutor during your spare period." She continued.

"Ok, I'll try not to waste their time." Jack replied, genuinely grateful for the help. Maybe this tutor would know how to help him focus and remember.

When Jack started high school he had high hopes. He wanted to be a doctor some day or an inventor and businessman inventing the next great thing. But then, the focus issues overcame him and changed his plans.

After the meeting they left the small office and said goodbye to the counsellor.

Jack walked back to the car. His head was down staring at his feet. He looked like he had just lost a popularity contest to a lamp.

They walked down the hall a little way and stopped.

Then, it happened - the moment that changed Jack's life.

His parents turned to him. His mom saw the defeat in his face and spoke first. "The way I see it Jack, you have two choices; you can give up and use this as an excuse for the rest of your life; or you can use this as an opportunity to prove the experts wrong."

"No one would blame you for giving up and not trying." She continued, "People will even help you complain for the rest of your life. No one will blame you for giving up and not trying so hard."

Jack listened, eager to hear what his mom would say next.

"Or you can choose to fight. You can use this moment as a challenge to try and prove them wrong - to show them that your future will not be decided by a test score."

Jack was speechless. He thought his life was over and now his parents are telling him the opposite. With motivating lines like that, his mother should really coach football. He thought about what his mom said, then replied.

"How can I change my brain? This is beyond my control. No matter what I do I can't change my brain!"

"Nothing is beyond your control. It's your life." his dad said.

His dad, a factory worker and machinist by trade, chimed in further. "I don't know anything about the brain, but I know every problem has a solution. If you can't overcome this, then you can learn from someone who has. You just need to find the solution."

Jack Smart had seen his dad, without any formal training, take a broken-down car and make it run like new again. When asked how he did it, he replied, "I just figured it out as I went."

He'd also seen his dad build a whole kitchen cabinet set from scratch, with no previous experience, and it looked better than expensive versions in the store. At work, Jack's dad had built airplane parts and even worked on part of the NASA Canada Robot Arm because he was one of the best machinists in the shop. Yet he only had a high school education. His motto was, "I'll just make it work." He had the fundamental belief that every problem had a solution. To his dad, the brain was just another machine.

Jack closed his eyes and thought. He imagined his whole life spread out in front of him, and the two paths he could follow. One path he imagined trying hard and looking for a solution to his memory problems. He would probably fail. Then he saw the other path where he lowered his expectations to avoid disappointment. Jack voiced his conclusion.

"Well If I give it my best try and fail," Jack pondered, "at least I know I tried. But if I quit now, I'll never know what I could have done."

"Jack be nibble, Jack be quick"

That night, Jack went home and started looking for brain training solutions.

Most of what he saw consisted of games to play. Somehow, he knew these games were a useless fad. If playing games improved memory then he would already have a great memory because of all the video games he played. And Jack was right.

With a little research he discovered that most Brain Games are criticised by neuroscientists because they only help you get better at playing the games. They don't actually improve the brain. He needed to figure out how the brain worked. He needed a manual for memory and focus.

After a bit more research, Jack found the World Memory Tournament Federation™, founded by a top expert on memory. Several other memory trainers and experts, from science and education, were listed as contributing partners and organizers. It almost looked too good to be true.

The art of memory, Jack learned, consists of a series of techniques that allow an ordinary person to achieve super human memorization abilities. Jack had heard of people memorizing a book word for word or mastering several languages in a short time or even cool things like memorizing decks of cards but he had always thought they were born with a natural gift. As he registered on the site and started looking into the history of memory, he realised the amazing truth. Memory is a skill not a talent.

These super human people who can memorize and recall anything at will are not born with special genes, but they practice an ancient art that has been passed down from teacher to student, through the generations. People skilled in this art often helped shape human history, from Chinese and Roman emperors to Alexander the Great, Leonardo da Vinci and JFK, this art was the secret weapon to great leaders in history.

Today the art is broken up into a Sport Memory and Practical Memory Skills. The sport is basic and easy to start with while the practical techniques are combined with modern neuroscience, and meant for the real world applications. Jack saw that there were more memory techniques today that the ancients never thought of - from understanding how memory is formed in the brain, to the ability to activate focus instantly, this system was exciting.

Jack decided this was the solution for him. Someone had discovered the manual to run the human brain. He clicked on the first lesson that promised to triple his memory.

Jack Smart is a fictional character based on Dave Farrow's experience in school. He's just a regular kid placed in real world situations to show how memory techniques work. If Jack Smart can do it, so can you!

Chapter 2

How Do I Triple My Memory Right Now?

Basic Memory Technique:
The Linking Method - by Dave Farrow

At this point you may be thinking, "Hey you have a great memory but I have a terrible memory."

Take heart! I teach people like you every day in my workshops and courses around the world. There is no such thing as a bad memory, just a bad technique.

Memory Test:

Do you have a favourite movie?

If you do, then think of it right now...yes that's right, stop reading for a moment and think of your favourite movie or any movie you like.

Write it down.

My Favorite Movie:

_____

If you had to take a test on the movie how would you do?

How much of that movie do you remember?

I've quizzed people for years and still find that most people can remember up to 90% of the movie. They can remember most of the movie they saw, even months or years later, as long as they like the movie and were paying some attention. My guess is that you are not far off from that.

Even if you only recall 70% of the movie content, think about how much information that is – the scenes, the costumes, the lines – there's a lot of information!

My next question is how hard did you have to work to memorize that movie?

How long did it take you?

It's a silly question! You memorized that movie in one repetition, as fast as you saw it!!

Did you need to have a great memory?

NO, of course not! The movie was memorable enough to stick in your head.

The fact is, your mind is not the problem. You already have a better than photographic memory. The problem is the information you are trying to recall and how you perceive it. I don't care who you are, if you don't have a serious brain injury or mental disease, then you do have an effective memory. Even if you have had a stroke, illness, or accident that has affected your memory, these techniques have been shown to help. I have seen it work. I have even worked with people suffering from a brain injury, with great success. And if they can do it, so can you. You just need to know how to use your memory.

Your Memory, Use It or Lose It

It's common knowledge in brain science that stimulating the memory works, and if you don't use it, you lose it. The power will fade. Your memory likes to get a workout. Many recent studies, including a study which I authored, have shown the power of the brain and its ability to achieve amazing feats of memory and focus.

You can achieve amazing recall using nothing more than simple memory strategies.

Don't confuse this with memory exercises or games, or rote memory. This is not just lifting a mental weight that only improves your memory by maybe 1% in a month. These are secret methods that people have used for thousands of years to achieve super human abilities of memory. These super brains have helped shape history, from Alexander the Great and Napoleon remembering the names of soldiers and the strategies to win, to the Cold War mentalist spies who used memory techniques to smuggle secrets across the Iron Curtain.

Today, memory training has taken a leap forward by incorporating modern neuroscience.

I call it **Memory 2.0.**

According to modern tests, the average human memory can recall 4-5 random objects after seeing them or hearing them only once.

A genius memory can recall 9-10 items. If you follow the instruction in this chapter, you will go from having a regular memory to having a genius level memory in minutes, just from taking this test.

How is this possible?

Well, your brain can't grow or change in minutes. Even **Brain Plasticity** takes time. The only way you can improve your memory in minutes is to use it differently. Think of it as the difference between pushing a car and getting in to drive it.

Here are the keys to your brain:

The Linking Method

I'm going to give you a list of twenty objects, and we're going to go through them one at a time. What I want you to do is to get your imagination going and get a little creative with me. Don't panic when you see the list, I will show you the secret way to easily memorize these objects.

Let's get started!

WMTF™ Manual

Here is the list of random objects:

1. Plane
2. Ice Cream
3. Whale
4. Diamond Ring
5. Computer
6. Snail
7. Fishing Pole
8. Clothes Hanger
9. Umbrella
10. Tower
11. Sailboat
12. Rocket
13. Grave
14. Robot
15. Earrings
16. Pitchfork
17. Swan
18. Axe
19. Swinging Patio Chair
20. Bowl of Salad

Don't try to memorize them yet. Follow the lesson first.

Follow along as I show you what goes on in my head when I memorize these random objects:

The first object in our list is a **Plane**.

Memory is simply the act of connecting information in the brain. The strength of your memory is the strength of the connections you can form between things.

The first item is a **Plane** and the second is an **Ice Cream**.

Here's where the fun begins!

In order to memorize anything, you must connect the first item to the next one. We are trying to tell our brain to connect the first item **Plane** to the second one, **Ice Cream**, even though there is no logical reason these two items should ever be in the same sentence.

Normally our brains try to reject connections like this because there is no logical reason that those two items should be connected. However, most of the information we need to memorize falls into this category.

Think about it.

There is no reason why my face should be called Dave any more than the little square brain in the computer should be called a CPU. It just is, and if we want to pass that next exam we need to remember it.

If our subconscious brains could talk they would be confused all the time because we want to connect all sorts of things together that have no logical connection. That's memory!

If it was logical we wouldn't need a good memory to do it. So what memory experts like me do, when we need to remember information, is to connect it on purpose.

How do we do this?

We make an image in our mind's eye, or in our imagination, that involves both things. Take item A and item B and imagine them in the same mental scene, involving all your senses if possible.

Don't just be visual. If you include other senses then it will work better. Immerse yourself in the scene.

Make it feel real.

But imagination alone is not strong enough...

Rarity

To connect information together, we imagine it in our mind's eye. I would imagine the **Ice Cream** sitting beside a **Plane**. That would be better than just reading the words on the page, and even work better than repetition, but it's still not a very strong memory until we add the last ingredient...Rarity.

I learned this concept from the great mentalist Harry Lorayne. The rarer and more unique something is, the more our brain pays attention. For years scientists thought memory experts could remember a lot of information just because they visualized it but that is only half the story. My Double Blind Study on **Memory Modes** proved that memory tricks only work when you make the image interesting and rare *to you*. That is your mode.

So let's go back to the **Plane** and the **Ice Cream**. Remember, we want to make it interesting. What do I mean by this?

Well, if you imagined a **Plane** delivering **Ice Cream**, you'd remember that for a minute or so, and if you actually saw it, you'd remember that for a little longer. But let me ask you something…if you imagined a **Plane** crashing into a giant **Ice Cream** cone, you'd remember that for a lot longer, right?

So take a moment now, and actually imagine a **Plane** crashing into an **Ice Cream** cone. Remember to close your eyes if you need to, to really get a vivid picture in your mind's eye. You're going to remember this picture for a very long time.

If that image doesn't work for you then you might have a different **Memory Modality** than me. So you might imagine an **Ice Cream** cone flying the **Plane**. You could imagine a **Plane** giving free **Ice Cream** to all its passengers.

The point is you can make your own image and if it is rare *to you* then you will remember it.

Back to the list; so far we have a plan to imagine each item in the list and make it rare or unique. Now, were almost ready to triple your memory.

After you make your image with the **Plane** and **Ice Cream** you can stop thinking about the **Plane**. You have connected it powerfully to the **Ice Cream** so you don't need to visualize it again.

Next, if we associate something else to the **Ice Cream**, suddenly, we have the start of a chain in our mind's eye that we cannot break.

At this point you may be thinking that this is crazy! And you'd be right. The very craziness of this technique is what makes sure that it sticks in your mind.

As you continue your journey of memory, you will learn more about what your brain finds rare and interesting.

In my science work, I observed this subject while working with thousands of people over decades. Different people will have different concepts of uniqueness. I was even able to prove in a lab that there are **5 different Memory Modes**. Each one actually activates the brain's memory centers differently.

For example, some people will like action and others will like fantasy. If you like action, you would imagine the **Plane** crashing into the **Ice Cream** and if you like fantasy, you would imagine the **Ice Cream** coming to life and flying into the **Plane**. This is an exciting new theory in neuroscience.

To find out more about **Memory Modes** go to **www.memorymodes.com** or visit the tournament website blog.

In the meantime, when you're doing this memory exercise, just imagine the first image that pops into your head. Also, challenge yourself by thinking of the craziest images you can.

Farrow Double Blind Study Results:

Students of the Farrow Method score 3 times higher than the control group on standard memory tests after only 20min of instruction, and tested a full week later.

Special thanks to Joe Makkerh and David Maillet at McGill University Neuroscience Dept. in Montreal for making this happen!

Triple Your Memory Exercise

Every time we mentally connect two objects together we call it a link. Below is a list of all the objects from the list you have to memorize.

The Rules: Your Mission should you chose to accept it is to think of the craziest image that will stick in your mind (everyone is different) for each link on the next page. Use my link descriptions as a guide but be creative and think of your own. Go quickly through the links and don't stop at any time. Many people have a timer running to keep them moving and test how long it takes. It doesn't matter how long you think of each image. Two seconds is fine. It matters how interesting the image is.

When you're ready to start, set the clock and turn the page

WMTF™ Manual

Each box has two items you need to mentally link together. Just link two items at a time, don't make one big picture in your mind, but make several little ones. This helps to keep the links separate and makes the chain more powerful.

Fill in the links for each pair in the chain and take a moment to imagine it in your mind's eye to make it stick.

Plane – Ice Cream	For this link I imagine a plane made of ice cream, or a plane crashing into a giant double scoop ice cream cone.
What do you imagine? _____ _____ _____ _____	
Ice Cream – Whale	I'd imagine a whale eating an ice cream cone or better yet, a whale swimming in ice cream! That's pretty unique, right?
What do you imagine? _____ _____ _____ _____	

Whale – Diamond Ring	I'd imagine millions of diamond rings coming out of the whale's blowhole. Can you imagine that? If you can imagine it, then you will remember it for a long time.
What do you imagine? _____ _____ _____ _____ _____	
Diamond Ring – Computer	I imagine someone putting a diamond ring around a computer or a computer getting married with a diamond ring on the mouse. Imagine one of these two pictures, or one of your own.
What do you imagine? _____ _____ _____ _____ _____	

Computer – Snail	I imagine a snail crawling across a computer keyboard and leaving a trail of slime. Imagine this in your mind's eye for just a moment.
What do you imagine? _____ _____ _____ _____	
Snail - Fishing Pole	An obvious image is a snail used as fishing bait BUT let's exaggerate it so we'll remember it better. I would imagine a giant Snail on the end of a fishing pole.
What do you imagine? _____ _____ _____ _____	

Fishing Pole – Coat Hanger	I would imagine using a coat hanger as a fishing pole. Imagine it clearly.
What do you imagine? _____ _____ _____	
Coat Hanger – Umbrella	Imagine an umbrella made out of coat hangers.
What do you imagine? _____ _____ _____	
Umbrella – Tower	Imagine jumping off of a tower and using an umbrella as a parachute on the way down. Don't actually do this. Just imagine it ok?
What do you imagine? _____ _____ _____	

Tower – Sailboat	I would imagine a stone tower built right in the middle of a giant sailboat. That would be a weird boat.
What do you imagine? _____	
Sailboat – Rocket	A rocket powered sailboat. I want one.
What do you imagine? _____	
Rocket – Grave	Imagine a rocket crashing into an open grave. Do they bury rockets?
What do you imagine? _____	

Grave – Robot	Coming to a theater near you - zombie robot attack! The robots are climbing out of a grave!
What do you imagine? _____ _____ _____ _____	
Robot – Earrings	How funny would an industrial robot look with makeup and giant earrings?
What do you imagine? _____ _____ _____ _____	
Earrings – Pitchfork	A pile of thousands of earrings is on the floor and I'm moving it with a pitchfork.
What do you imagine? _____ _____ _____ _____	

WMTF™ Manual

Pitchfork – Swan	I imagine a swan using a pitchfork. How crazy is that?!
What do you imagine? _____	
Swan – Axe	I imagine a swan chopping down a tree with an axe. How would he hold the axe?
What do you imagine? _____	
Axe – Patio Chair	I imagine just destroying the chair with an axe.
What do you imagine? _____	

Patio Chair – Salad	Spilling salad all over the chair and leaving it out overnight. Rotten salad chair. I'll remember that!
What do you imagine? _____ _____ _____ _____	

Recall

Now take a moment out just to review the first few items in your mind. If you visualized them in your mind's eye and followed the directions, then the answers should pop right into your head.

One helpful trick is to imagine the items one at a time. Instead of saying in your head "what's the next item" over and over, try imagining one item and the next one should jump into your mental picture. If not, just go back and make a better link that your brain likes better. With practice you will be able to do thousands.

So what did we start with?

Remember to visualize the item in your mind's eye and take a moment and write down all the items you remember. When you are finished flip the page. If you get stuck go to another part of the list and work backwards.

1. _____
2. _____
3. _____
4. _____
5. _____
6. _____
7. _____
8. _____
9. _____
10. _____
11. _____
12. _____
13. _____
14. _____
15. _____
16. _____
17. _____
18. _____
19. _____
20. _____

Evaluation: How Did You Do?

According to some I.Q. Tests, if you scored 5-6 items correctly you have an average memory. If you recalled 9-10 items correctly then you have a genius level memory. If got all of them right you're a Double Genius! This is not a real category on I.Q. Tests. Technically, most I.Q. Tests state that recalling 20 items on this test is way off the charts.

In memory training we call it a good start.

How to Eliminate Mistakes

When I recalled 59 Decks of cards for my Guinness Record I had to get under 0.5% mistakes to get the record. I only got one mistake. I won't hold you to that standard.

If you missed any items in the list, just follow the directions below. A mistake is usually due to one of two reasons:

1. The image you made was not visualized, or not visualized clearly enough. In this case, just review the link and make it clearer. Think of it like turning up the resolution in your mind; make the image brighter, clearer, closer, louder and more vivid. Closing your eyes may help.

2. The image you imagined was not interesting enough to you. You may have imagined the image I gave you and your brain had difficulty thinking of it. The best solution is to make your own link. The link you make will be the best one for you to remember.

Later you will use this same list that you just memorized to help you memorize an entire deck of cards!

If you haven't done it already, try going online to our website right now and follow along with the first lesson at: **www.memorytournament.com**

In the first lesson you will see images flash on the screen to help you associate information instead of just reading a description like you did in this book.

Next try this on your own or with your friends!

Don't use my links all the time. Use your own links and images to help you recall the list. Your skill will get better with more practice.

Try a Practice Game

Did you know that you can actually play a Memory Tournament Match right now with just the Linking Method? Grab a friend or use our computer simulation.

If you play with a friend, be fair and let them learn the list technique first!

Later in this book you will learn advanced techniques for things like cards and numbers but let's do one exercise now to see how a memory game works

The **Basic Rules** are on the next page!

Basic Game

Pre-Match Memorizing Round: Step by Step

It takes three people to play: a judge and two players.

One person acts as the judge and sets a timer for a minute or two of memorization time (depending on how long the players agree they need).

The Judge starts the clock and the two players focus on the **Monumentum™** trying to memorize the row or group of information on the page. (See next page for Monumentum™ description). When the timer stops, the judge ends the **Memorizing Round** and the players must stop.

The Recall Match: Step by Step

1. Flip a coin or use paper rock scissors to determine the starting player.

2. Player #1 will state the first item in the **Monumentum™** list.

3. Player #2 will counter by saying the second item in the list and the game is on. Back and forth, the players say the next item in the list until one player makes a mistake. The first mistake signals a stop to the **Recall Match**.

4. The player who did not make the mistake is the winner for this round. Players can continue with more rounds and more players. See **Chapter 8** for complete rules and variations!

Congratulations on your very first Memory Tournament Match!

The Monumentum™

A **Monumentum**™ is the official information that Memory Club Players memorize during the game. It sits in the middle of the table between the players.

The term Monumentum™ comes from a Latin word that means a recording for the purpose of remembrance. It is where we get the word monument.

Monuments are often huge structures that only serve the purpose to help us remember something important in the past like a battle or invention. It is the oldest form of memory technique. At the World Memory Tournament Federation™ we also see memory games as a monumental, memory challenge.

Any information can be used as a Monumentum™ such as random numbers, foreign language vocabulary, study notes, technical terms and scripture, but only official Tournament Federation Monumentum™ forms will be allowed for competition and ranking.

Monumentums™ are found in your club kit or online at: **www.memorytournament.com**

"Even one mistake can Cost you a match. In this way, the Memory Tournament cannot be won, it can only be lost."
- Dave Farrow

Chapter 3

Sport Memory and Practical Memory

Beyond Sport, Memory 2.0 - by Dave Farrow

Today, memory training falls into two categories: **Sport Memory** and **Practical Memory Skills**.

Sport Memory:

When you train in a Memory Tournament Club there are three main categories in which you can practice and compete: **Word Lists, Numbers and Playing Cards**.

Other information or categories can be used for memorizing in the games, but we start here because these three categories represent pure memory skills, and also cross all cultural barriers. People from all around the world and all ages can play on an even playing field in tournaments with word lists, numbers and playing cards.

We also start by teaching these skills because they form a good basis to grow as a memory student. It is also exciting to watch, it's riveting to see two players go back and forth recalling numbers one at a time. As they take turns, each says the next number, card or word in the sequence, the tension builds. Will one player make a mistake? How many items can they recall before one of them makes a mistake? As the number of items passes 30 then 40, it becomes impossible to look away!

The first one to make a mistake loses.

The techniques used to compete in a memory tournament are very simple effective tools for stretching the brain. It's a great way to start with the basics, but they have limited application in the real world. There aren't many times when you need to memorize a 1000 digit number in the real world!

The downside is that Sport Memory techniques like the Journey Method don't create as powerful a mental link as long term memory techniques. Therefore they are not as effective for studying. They are great for cramming and recalling information on the same day, but if you want to learn a skill, language or master a profession, accuracy and long term memory are the most important factors and are only found in **Practical Memory Skills**.

Our goal is to hook young people and adults alike with the exciting sport of memory. Later on, show them the advanced, practical techniques they can use in the real world to study better and be successful in life.

The techniques in this book will show your club members how to easily memorize hundreds, even thousands of numbers, cards or words in a row.

Once a new player discovers how to do these amazing feats of memory, there is an instant urge to see how far and fast one can go. You will want to pit your skills against others. Thus the Memory Tournament is born!

Enjoy the new sport of memory, learn the basics, and when you're ready to go to the next level with practical memory, you can raise money for your club by hosting a Memory Workshop approved by the **World Memory Tournament Federation™**. A list of Certified Memory Instructors can be found on our website.

By hosting a Memory Workshop you can raise money for your own memory club or for another group or charity. You can give back to the community and share your new memory knowledge. Family and friends can attend the workshop and learn the real world applications of memory science. You may even get more members to attend your club!

Practical Memory:

There isn't much demand in the real world for a person who can memorize a 1000 digit number or 1000 random words. Outside of a casino floor, memorizing a deck of cards isn't in high demand either. These game-based memory skills are the basic building blocks for more practical, real life memory skills.

As mentioned earlier, the Sport Memory techniques focus on memorizing information and recalling in the same day. Practical Memory skills are designed for the real world and they give the student the ability to remember vast amounts of information for the rest of their lives, making a dramatic impact on their grades and future.

In the real world, information can be messy and complex. Real learning and raising grades involves a variety of mental skills. This includes organizing information in the brain (called Information Matrix or Architecture) and focus techniques that allow students to instantly activate focus in the brain, at will, for more effective studying.

> "The failing student, who uses the memory club to turn around their grades, may become the next great inventor or healer. If we can catch students at the right time in life and teach them proper brain based learning methods, it will change the world."
> - Dave Farrow

Practical Memory Skills, sometimes called **Memory 2.0**, are a series of advanced techniques designed to be directly applied to real world applications. In the Practical Memory Workshop, students learn how to memorize hundreds of technical terms or definitions and organize them in their head so test taking becomes effortless. They learn how to turn the number technique into a skill to memorize formulas, math concepts, locations and more. Other techniques include: speeches, text, names, preventing brain fog, memory loss and forgetfulness, remembering names and faces, mentally organizing whole curriculums, improving focus and concentration, and much more.

The **Practical Memory Skills** allow the student to take their new **Sport Memory Skills** and apply them to studying, business, social situations and life.

Practical Memory skills also help people train their brains to stay sharper. In feedback from practical memory students, adults over 40 years old reported much less brain fog and mental fatigue. You experience less forgetfulness such as walking into a room and forgetting why you're there, or misplacing keys and glasses.

Many people today have turned to mental games to train the brain but this fad is not the best way to train the brain or improve memory. Many researchers comment that brain games will get you better at brain games but not much else.

To truly exercise and improve memory, people need to actually use their memory. Nothing else works. Only using your memory will strengthen it, and the using Practical Memory Skills is the best way to do this.

It's not every day you get asked to memorize the order of a deck of cards, however a Sport Memory student becomes a sponge for information and a genius at learning. This quest for improved sport memory ability leads to proficiency at the art of Practical Memory.

Most students cut study time by more than half and score higher on tests. Later in life, students have used the art of memory to truly stand out. One memory trainer I worked with learned 29 languages and practiced them fluently as a journalist. Another memorized a set of important books, word for word. Yet another person memorized all the product information in their job, amazed clients, and got promoted.

Even I used the powerful skills of memory to achieve great things. With heightened focus and improved memory, I became a Nano-tech Scientist and Consultant. I learned auto-CAD and became a 3D Designer and self-taught Design Engineer. I even became my own Publicist. I've been hired by major pharmaceutical and automobile companies to design new products and I've also invented my own products and brought them to market. All the while, I have been on the cutting edge of memory and brain training science. None of this would be possible without the skills of memory training.

The world is changing fast and the ability to learn new skills on the job and in the field is quickly becoming the highest priority in the workplace too. A world of opportunity opens up to the individual who can learn any new skill and master it quickly.

To get started, I recommend you start with a **World Memory Tournament Federation™ Club** to get the basics and get others involved. When you're ready to apply memory techniques to studying and other real world applications, you can contact your **Regional Coordinator** and ask to host a Memory Workshop with a Certified Memory Instructor at your club or school.

During the workshop, the instructor teaches the audience through real world examples and applications of memory techniques: remembering names and faces, cutting study time, memorizing technical terms or large amounts of information, remembering formulas, expanding your vocabulary, learning musical notes or how to play an instrument, learning new software, learning industry information, and even foreign languages. These are just a few of the ways that memory training can help you in your life. These skills allow you to learn real world job and academic skills with no frustration and in a fraction of the time it will take for others.

By hosting a memory workshop at your location, you can raise money for your club and even get your club or group recognized in the local media. Clubs often earn thousands of dollars which they can apply to scholarships, charities or club uniforms.

Contact your **Regional Coordinator** to learn how you can raise money for your club while helping your community.

Or email us directly at:
info@memorytournament.com

If you can't host a WMTF™ approved Memory Workshop and certified Instructor, you can check our calendar at **www.memorytournament.com** for a memory event or workshop in your area.

If you prefer to learn at your own pace, in your own home, you can check out our product page and purchase an affordable Certified Memory Training Program.

Just remember to only use Certified Memory Instructors and Programs approved by the World Memory Tournament Federation™. Avoid copycats and imitations.

If you don't or can't have a memory workshop at your club, another way were bringing Practical Memory to people is through an accountability buddy.

This is an idea that Life Hacker Sergio Gonzales came up with. Say you want to learn Italian and you want to use your memory club to help you. Simply find a buddy in the club that will aim for the same goal with you or has another goal they want to achieve. You can play tournaments to memorize vocabulary and compete against each other to help achieve your goal in a fun way.

We also encourage you to write down your goal and give it to your buddy with clear achievements that you're holding yourself to each week. People always work harder when they know they'll have to face their accountability buddy at the next meeting.

We have a number of tools to help you achieve your goals on the website. Try out our lesson plans for use in the classroom and specific Monumentums™ for different subjects like languages.

For more information, email us at **clubs@memorytournament.com**

In just one hour, a Certified Memory Instructor can help you raise test scores while cutting study time and frustration.

WORLD MEMORY **TOURNAMENT** FEDERATION

Chapter 4

What is the Journey Method?

Memorizing Long Sequences of Information
By Chester Santos - US Memory Champion

We are now going to learn my favorite memory improvement technique. It's the tool that I've used most often over the years while competing in memory competitions. The technique is very powerful and probably the most easily extensible of all of the techniques covered in this manual. Once mastered, it will allow you to build up an endless supply of mental filing cabinets.

This particular technique has a very long history and has been known by a number of different names. It seems to have originated with the ancient Greeks, and was known as the *method of loci*. It was later used by the Roman orators to memorize long speeches and texts, and became known as the *Roman Room method*. Nowadays, it is used by modern memorizers like myself, and is often referred to as the *Journey Method*.

The Journey Method utilizes both sides of your brain to encode information, and involves linking vivid mental imagery to an ordered sequence of locations with which you are familiar.

For example, you could use locations from your residence, grocery store, favorite mall, friend's place, local gym, etc. The first step is to learn the locations in order, and be able to mentally traverse them in sequence. In order to help you get a feel for what a journey is, and the types of locations that a typical journey can contain, I'm going to walk you through one that I've used many times throughout the years in competitions.

I often use my apartment and imagine walking through it and looking at the following locations in order: front door, cupboard, refrigerator, stove, kitchen sink, microwave, television, coffee table, couch, easy chair, bedroom mirror, closet, bathroom sink, bathtub, toilet, bedroom lamp, window sill, head of the bed, foot of the bed, and dresser. You will notice that there are 20 different locations along my journey. Every time I use this particular "apartment journey", I mentally traverse the 20 locations in the same sequence every time. This allows me to memorize information in order.

Once you know the order of the locations, you can then link vivid imagery to each location. Again, the vivid imagery will represent the information that you want to remember. I'm going to teach you the Journey Method by having you go through a fun exercise that will not only give you a good handle on using the journey method, but that will also illustrate just how powerful everything that you've learned so far really is. Shortly, you are going to be able to quickly and easily memorize and perfectly recall 20 years worth of Academy Award Winners for Best Picture!

WMTF™ Manual

The first step is to establish a journey. Using my example as a guide, I want for you to choose 20 locations from your residence and learn them in order. The sequence of the locations should be natural. In other words, you should learn them in the order in which you would encounter them if you were going to take a certain route around your residence. Please make sure that you can mentally traverse through each location on your journey, in the same order, at least a few times before continuing to the next paragraph.

Now that you've established a journey and are able to mentally traverse it in order, we are going to use it to memorize the following list of Academy Award Winners for Best Picture:

1988 – Rainman
1989 – Driving Miss Daisy
1990 – Dances with Wolves
1991 – Silence of the Lambs
1992 – The Unforgiven
1993 – Schindler's List
1994 – Forrest Gump
1995 – Braveheart
1996 – The English Patient
1997 – Titanic
1998 – Shakespeare in Love
1999 – American Beauty
2000 – Gladiator
2001 – A Beautiful Mind
2002 – Chicago
2003 – Lord of the Rings
2004 – Million Dollar Baby
2005 – Crash
2006 – The Departed
2007 – No Country for Old Men.

1. At your first location, I want for you to imagine that you see Dustin Hoffman taking a bunch of toothpicks out of the location. He's dropping them on the floor and compulsively counting them. Really try to see and even hear all of this happening in your mind. In addition to seeing him counting the toothpicks, you notice that it's raining all over him, because he is "Rainman". With this funny little scenario and the others to follow, just relax and enjoy picturing them.

2. At your next location, you see a little daisy. This daisy is not like any other flower that you've ever seen. It's wearing a skirt and actually has eyes, a nose, mouth, and ears. Even more surprising, is the fact that this daisy is now speaking to you! She is telling you that she her name is Miss Daisy, and you now notice that she is wearing a skirt! All of a sudden, Miss Daisy gets into a car and starts driving all over your second location. Think of the scenario that you've just witnessed as being "Driving Miss Daisy".

3. At your third location, you see a pack of scary looking wolves! They are glaring at you, growling, and showing their teeth! You feel really scared! But suddenly, without warning, the wolves start to smile and one by one they start to do a little dance! You can't help but marvel at seeing each one of the wolves do its own unique little dance. You were scared of them at first, but now they are entertaining you with their dancing. Think of this funny little scenario as being "Dances with Wolves".

WMTF™ Manual

4.   At your next location, you see a large group of little lambs. They are moving around and bah-ing loudly. They just keep going on and on: "Bah! Bah! Bah!" The bah-ing is getting so loud that it starts to hurt your ears. But suddenly and unexpectedly, the lambs fall on the ground with their eyes closed and just go completely silent! You wonder if maybe they are dead, but all you know for certain is that they are now silent and not making any sounds whatsoever. Think of that scenario as being "Silence of the Lambs".

5.   There is a priest with his torso sticking out of your next location! You have no idea what this priest could be doing there and why in the world his torso would be sticking out of that location of your journey. Below him, you notice a sign that says "Confessions being taken today". You decide to ask him if you can be forgiven. Big mistake. The priest starts yelling at you, continuosly screaming "You are the unforgiven!". Think of that disturbing little scenario as being "The Unforgiven".

6.   There are a bunch of shins pasted on your next location! You examine each shin and notice that each one has a list written on it. You wonder to yourself what this list could possibly be for. Think of that scenario as being "Schindler's List".

7.   At your next location, you see Forrest Gump (Tom Hanks)! He has a collection of chocolate boxes, and keeps offering you one. Forrest Gump keeps asking, "Would you like a box of chocolates?" You finally decide to go ahead and accept his offer. When you open the box, out sprouts a chocolate forest! Think of this unusual and funny scenario as being "Forrest Gump".

8.   Waiting for you at your next location is Mel Gibson from Braveheart! His face is painted blue and he is yelling loudly about freedom! He keeps pounding his chest and tells you that if you want freedom, you'd better have a very brave heart! Really try to see and hear this happening at this location on your journey, and think of it as being "Braveheart".

9.   At your next location, you see a man surrounded by a team of doctors. Why is he surrounded by doctors? Because he is a patient! You hear the patient talking to the doctors and notice that he has an English accent. Of course, this is because he is "The English Patient"!

10.   At the next location on your journey, you see something really unusual! It looks like a tiny model of The Titanic, but there appear to be real people inside of it. The Titanic is moving along the location on your journey, but it runs into an iceberg! You can see all of the tiny people jumping out of the ship and you can hear them screaming. Of course, think of this scenario as being "Titanic".

11.   A man is standing at your next location. You think to yourself, how in the world did he get in here? He's dressed in Shakespearean era type clothing and is reading poetry. He's reading the poetry and seems to be very emotional about it. Why is he doing this? Because he's in love! Think of this scenario as being "Shakespeare in Love".

12.   At the next location along your journey, you see a very beautiful woman. She appears to be dressed as a beauty contest contestant. You see her posing and showing off her figure. She now even seems to be trying to flirt with you! Across her chest, you see a banner that reads "American Beauty". Think of her and this scenario as being "American Beauty".

13.   At your next location, you see a gladiator. He is trying to pry out a shield, sword, and ball of chain, each of which you see lodged into the location on your journey. You ask him what he is doing and he tells you that he is preparing for battle, because he is a gladiator! Of course, think of this scenario as being "Gladiator".

14.   You are sort of grossed out at first by what you see at your next location. It looks like a giant brain. For some strange reason though, you feel compelled to think of it as a "mind" and you examine it further. There is something beautiful about its shape and form. You start to think of it as being a very beautiful mind, and even start to stroke it. It feels really strange. Think of that scenario as being "A Beautiful Mind".

15.   You are really excited by what you see at your next location! It's a Chicago style pizza! Yummy! You take a slice and start to scarf it down. Delicious! Think of this as being "Chicago".

16.   At your next location, you see a strange ring. It's glowing! All of a sudden, a man puts on the ring. The man starts to glow as well! The ring on his hand suddenly splits into many rings! The man starts to speak to you in an eerie voice and tells you that he is The Lord of the Rings!

17.   There is a baby crawling around on your next location! This baby is wearing a diaper filled with cash! My goodness, you think to yourself, that must be about a million dollars stuffed into that baby's diaper! As the baby crawls around, you see the cash start to spew from his diaper. Think of that baby as being the "Million Dollar Baby".

18.   At your next location, there are a bunch of what appear to be model cars. The cars are facing each other and revving their engines. All of a sudden, they drive at each other at full speed and there is a huge crash! It's the loudest and most explosive crash that you've ever witnessed. Think of that scenario as being "Crash".

19.   Your next location is lined with coffins. This is so strange and eerie! Even though you are a bit weirded-out, you decide to open one of the coffins. Sure enough, inside you find one of the departed! Think of that whole experience as being "The Departed".

20.   At the final location on your journey, you see a group of old men. They are all chained up, struggling to get free. There is a menacing looking figure torturing them. You can hear the villain yelling at them continuously, "This is no country for old men!" Think of that scenario as being "No Country for Old Men".

If you were able to clearly visualize and experience those scenarios in your mind at each location along your journey, then you should now be able to recall the last 20 Best Picture winners by merely thinking of each location on your journey.

Knowing that we started with the winner in 1988, you now know that in 1988 Rainman won the Academy Award for Best Picture. Who won in 1990? In order to answer that question, just mentally go to the third location on your journey. The scenario with the wolves should come back to your mind and you'll know that Dances with Wolves won the Academy Award for Best Picture in 1990. This is really amazing, isn't it? I hope that you are enjoying yourself and seeing the power what you are learning.

The exercise that you've just gone through, illustrates how to put together many of the things that you've learned in this manual. It shows you that the tools that you've learned can be applied to learning much more than just random words, but actually **any** type of information that you want to remember. You merely need to create an image or series of images that represent the information that you want to remember, and then link those images to locations that you are familiar with.

As you practice the journey method, along with all of the other techniques that you've learned in this manual, you'll begin to notice an improvement in your ability to quickly and easily create vivid images and scenarios in your mind. In addition, you will start to notice that you are able to see the images in your mind more clearly. The images will become clearer and more lifelike. At that point, you will know that some real physical changes have occurred in your brain. You will have built up some, what we could call, "mental muscle." Along with your increased visualization ability, will come a stronger and more powerful imagination. At that time, your skills will have reached the point to where you will have the ability to actually create your own *purely imaginary* journeys. That is to say, that you will be able create journeys that exist solely in your mind, but not in the real world.

For instance, you might imagine a castle. The castle begins with drawbridge. After the drawbridge, you reach a giant castle door. When you open the door, there is a long red carpet. The red carpet leads to a staircase, etc... As you mentally review the castle that you've created with your imagination, it will eventually become a real place in your mind. Then you will be able to use that imaginary castle and the locations within it to store images and information, just like you learned to do with a journey along a real world location such as your residence. This type of advanced memory technique was actually used by the Chinese at some point in their history to memorize ancient texts. They called the purely imaginary journeys, Memory Palaces.

You now have a very solid foundation in the fundamentals of memory improvement. The techniques that you've learned in this manual will allow you to dramatically improve your memory. As with anything else in life, the more you practice, the better you will get and the more improvement you will see. As you can no doubt tell from going through the exercises, practicing these techniques is also wonderful exercise for your brain. Congratulations on beginning your journey towards a powerful memory and lifelong mental fitness!

Chapter 5

How Do I Memorize Numbers?

Phonetic Alphabet System
By Chester Santos - US Memory Champion

You are about to learn the most powerful and effective system for memorizing numbers that has ever been created. The system was developed over 300 years ago by *Stanislaus Mink von Wennsshein and is commonly referred to as the Phonetic Alphabet System, Major System, and the Phonetic Mnemonic System.*

This manual will refer to it as the *Phonetic Alphabet System*. In this system, each number between 0 and 9 has one or more phonetic consonant sound(s) associated with it. This is illustrated in the chart below:

The first column gives you the sounds associated with each number. The second column gives you the number. The third column gives you some hints and associations to help you mentally link each number to its corresponding sounds.

Sometimes a hint is only given for one of the sounds associated with a particular number and not for the others, but that should be enough, because all of the sounds associated with a particular number sound very similar to each other, and those sounds are also formed in the same exact way with your mouth and tongue.

Sounds	Number	Hints/Associations
s,z	0	(z)er0
t,d	1	1 downstroke in each letter
n	2	2 downstrokes in the letter
m	3	3 downstrokes in the letter
r	4	fou(r)
l	5	pointer finger and thumb form "L" shape if left hand held up for high-five
ch,sh,j	6	the number 6, if written with a small loop, looks like the mirror image of the letter "J"
k,g	7	if the letter "K" is written like the Kellogg's "K", it looks like it contains two 7's
f,v	8	if you write out a lowercase cursive "f", you will notice that the two loops form an 8
p,b	9	if you write out the number 9 reversed or upside down, it looks like a "p" or a "b"

WMTF™ Manual

In other words, your mouth and tongue will be in the same exact position when producing the "z" sound and the "s" sound. You learned the phonetic sounds for each of the 26 letters in the English language when you were learning to read in English.

I'll now quickly give you a more detailed explanation of the hints and associations given in the third column of the chart:

If you write out the word "zero" and say it out loud, it's clear that it begins with the "z" sound and also that the word ends in an "O" (easily associated with the number 0). This will help to make a link in your mind between the "z" sound and the number 0. The "s" sound just sounds very similar.

If you write out a lowercase letter "t" or "d", how many times will your pen or pencil make a down stroke? The answer is "1" or that your pen or pencil will only make a downward motion one time. Give it a try and count. This will help to make a link in your mind between the "t" and "d" sounds and the number 1.

If you write out a lowercase letter "n", how many times will your pen or pencil make a down stroke? The answer is "2" or that your pen or pencil will make a downward motion two times. Give it a try and count. This will help to make a link in your mind between the "n" sound and the number 2.

If you write out a lowercase letter "m", how many times will your pen or pencil make a down stroke? The answer is "3" or that your pen or pencil will make a downward motion three times. Give it a try and count. This will help to make a link in your mind between the "m" sound and the number 3.

If you write out the word "four" and say it loud, it will become clear to you that the word "four" ends very clearly with the "r" sound. This will help to make a link in your mind between the "r" sound and the number 4.

If you hold up your left hand, as if you were about to give someone a "high-five", you can clearly see an "L" shape formed with by your index finger and thumb. This will help to make a link in your mind between the "L" sound and the number 5.

If you write out the number "6" with a small thin loop forming sort of a hook shape as some people make their "6's", it will then look very similar to a mirror image of the letter "J" which also has a hook shape. This will help to make a link in your mind between the "J" sound and the number 6. The "ch" and "sh" sounds just sound very similar.

If you write out a large letter "K" similar to how the large red "K" on the Kellogg's cereal box appears, you will be able to see that the "K" is actually formed from two "7's". One "7" on the left, and another "7" on the right. Basically, two "7's" can be joined together in a certain way to form the letter "K". Go ahead and give it a try. This will help to make a link in your mind between the "K" sound and the number 7. The "g" sound just sounds very similar. It's important to note the "g" sound here is the hard "g" sound as in the words "gas" and "game". The soft "g" sound as in the words "gel" or "giraffe" correspond to the number 6 because that's actually the "J" sound.

If you write out a lowercase cursive "f", you'll notice that the two loops in the middle form what look like an "8". Give it a try and see. This will help to make a link in your mind between the "f" sound and the number 8.

If you take the number "9" and flip it around, it forms the letter "p". Go ahead and write out a "9" and then imagine simply flipping it over. If you were then to take the "p" and flip it up, you would see that it forms a "b". Basically, different orientations of a "9" form the letters "p" and b". This will help to make a link in your mind between the "p" and "b" sounds and the number 9.

Take about 15 minutes or so to familiarize yourself with the chart above using the hints and associations I've given to guide you.
Once you become familiar with the system, you will be able to form words to represent number sequences. From the words, you can create images and see them in your mind.

For example, for the number 14, you could picture a tire (1(t)--i--4(r)--e). As you can see, you can use vowels anywhere you'd like when coming up with words to represent a number sequence.

The number 57 could be represented by an image of a log (5(l)--o--7(g)). When mastering this system, it is important to understand that the sounds are what matter, not the letters. For instance, the number 76 could be represented by an image of a cage (7(k-sound)--a--(j-sound)--e).

Before continuing, study the phonetic alphabet system chart until you feel comfortable with it.

Now that you are comfortable with the system, let's go over some practical applications. There were 126, 250 hybrid cards sold in the US last year. How can you easily commit this fact to memory? You can do so by imagining a hybrid car that has a danish (1(d)--a--2(n)--i--6(sh)) in place of a steering wheel. The danish is filled with nails (2(n)--a--i--5(l)--0(s)).

If you can vividly experience the image in your mind, then you will remember the fact. For example, really try to imagine that you enter a hybrid car and are very surprised to see a danish in place of the steering wheel. You try to use the danish as a steering wheel but prick your fingers on the nails. Ouch! If this were a fact that you needed to recite during a presentation for work or school, once you think of hybrid cars, the vivid imagery would come back to you, and once you know the phonetic alphabet system well, you'd know for certain that this imagery means that 126, 250 hybrid cars were sold in the US last year! This is very powerful stuff!

What if you needed to remember that your doctor's phone number is 357-4782? You could simply imagine a stethoscope (to represent doctor) wrapped around a milk (3(m)--i--5(l)--7(k)) covered rock (4(r)--o--7(k-sound)), which is smashing up a fan (8(f)--a--2(n)). If you vividly experience this happening in your mind, and you know the phonetic alphabet system, then the next time you think of your doctor, the image beginning with the stethoscope will come back to you, and you will know that the phone number is 357-4782!

Besides the fact that it is incredibly useful and impressive to be able to remember facts that contain figures, doing so is also wonderful exercise for your brain! If you would like a really effective brain workout, try memorizing long number sequences.

Take the following 20 digit sequence:

13492227468279749230

Such a sequence can easily be memorized by placing an image at each of 10 locations along a journey. You learned the Journey Method in a previous chapter of this manual. Simply break the number sequence into 10 images and have each image interact in an interesting way in your mind with the corresponding location of your journey. The sequence above could be turned into the following 10 images: Tom (13), rope (49), nun (22), Nick (27), Rich (46), fan (82), cop (79), car (74), bun (92), mouse (30). So, you could then visualize someone named Tom interacting with the first location of your journey, then a rope interacting with your journey's second location, a nun interacting with the third location, and so on...

Once you've placed the 10 images at the 10 corresponding locations of your journey, you simply need to then think of your locations in order and see what images you placed at each one. Each image will correspond to a specific 2 digit sequence. That will give you the entire 20 digit sequence in order!

Enjoy using the Phonetic Alphabet System to develop your ability to remember numbers! Doing so will help you to accomplish things that you may have previously thought impossible.

Chapter 6

How to Memorize a Deck of Cards

Farrow Method Card Technique©
By Dave Farrow

Now that you can memorize objects by visualizing them in your mind's eye, what if I told you that each one of the objects you memorized earlier in the manual represented a card?

That means that you just memorized the order of 20 cards in a row!

Here's How:

In order to memorize cards you must be able to visualize them just like you did with the list. The way I do this is to create what's called a Peg List.

Think of your mind like a wall and all the information in the world as coats or jackets that you can hang on the wall. However, your mental wall was not made with enough hooks, so most of the information you try to hang on it, falls to the floor and is forgotten.
By placing a hook or peg on the wall, it acts as a connection between the wall and the coat. In the same way, using a mental peg will act as a hook between your mind and the information you want to remember. It works really well if done right, and is perfect for this situation. The cards are like the coats without hooks; if left to their own devices they would not stick in your mind. But if you have a code that turns the cards into

objects (for example, Queen of Diamonds means a Diamond Ring), then you could link them to your mind just like you did with the list in the previous chapter. How do we make this code, you ask?

The first code I used for memorizing cards translated the cards into words using the phonetic alphabet. But it took several steps and took me at least 60 days of practice before they came to me like second nature. Others swear by this code, but I did not like it.

Other people have used codes with celebrities represented by each card and others still use actions or their own personalized codes and links.

When I started to teach the technique to memorize cards, I wanted a code that you could learn instantly. I wanted to teach someone in less than an hour how to memorize a deck of cards. After some effort I fell upon this idea and today it is the fastest way to learn card memory techniques. You will need advanced techniques to be the fastest card memorizer but this will get you to memorizing a deck of cards quicker than any other method.

The Farrow Method Card Technique© was first published in 1999 as *The 6 Minute Deck©*. This book was designed to teach magicians how to memorize a deck of cards in under six minutes. In actuality, it took less time but people responded to the 6 minute idea because there was a book called the *Six Hour Deck* out on shelves at the same time. Needless to say, this book was popular in some circles.

The Visual Peg List

I like the direct approach. The problem is simple: every time I see a card, it needs to remind me of an object or item that's easier to remember than cards.

The problem with cards is that each card consists of both a number and a suit.

If I need to think of an object every time I see a card then I want to see the card and have it instantly remind me of the object.

For this reason, a visual code is the easiest to learn because of the **Eidetic Memory** quality. There's no need to go through the extra step of learning the code, if it's automatic.

Eidetic Memory is sometimes called **Engram Memory** and means something that is written firmly on the brain. It usually refers to a situation where it is easy to remember information after seeing it just once. This code I developed does just that. You just need to see it once and "boom" it hits your brain like a fist and you never forget the link. At least that's the plan.

How is this possible you might ask?

Well, simply by being direct! Instead of making a code that turns the numbers into sounds, and the suits into something else, and making a big list, I just got creative. I looked at the card (the top left hand corner to be exact) and drew a picture out of the elements in the corner of the card. That is why the Queen of Diamond is a Diamond Ring in my code, because when you look at it in the right way it looks like a diamond ring!

Take a look at the image on the left. If you use your imagination you can see the Diamond ring in your mind's eye. The picture on the right is to help you see the connection.

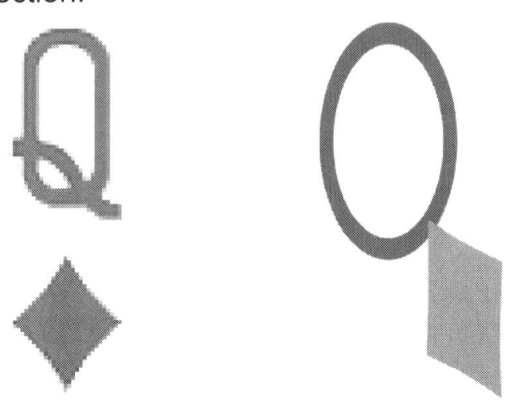

Let's try this exercise with some other cards.

The Jack of Clubs looks like a fishing hook stuck in clovers.

You can think of something else if you like. You might not fish or just not like my images. That's fine, but don't over think it too much.

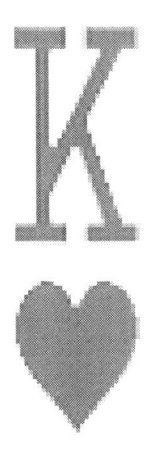

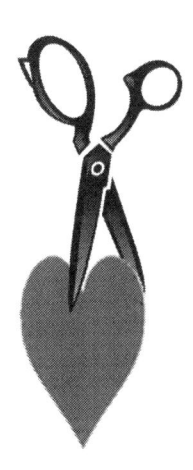

Here's how I see the King of Hearts!

As you can see, the pictures look like the cards do. In a few cases, I had to turn a card around or move some of the pieces, but all in all, this code is very natural.

The success of this code lies in this fact: whenever I teach this to people, they learn it in a couple of hours.

Engram Memory

As I said before, an Engram is an old word meaning to write on the brain. It usually refers to some traumatic event that you just can't seem to forget, but it also applies loosely to that jingle you hear on the radio that you just can't get out of your head.

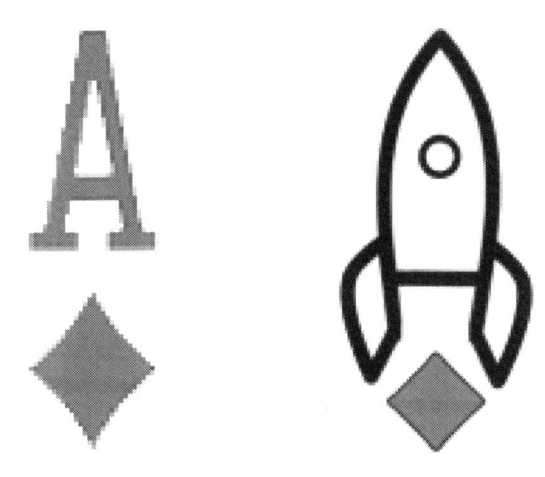

Think about it - once you look at the Ace of Diamonds above and see the Rocket Ship, it's hard not to see it the next time you see the card. That's the idea. I want this to be like second nature for you.

The entire list is on the next few pages...

Spades

The Ace of Spades looks like a jet landing on an airstrip.

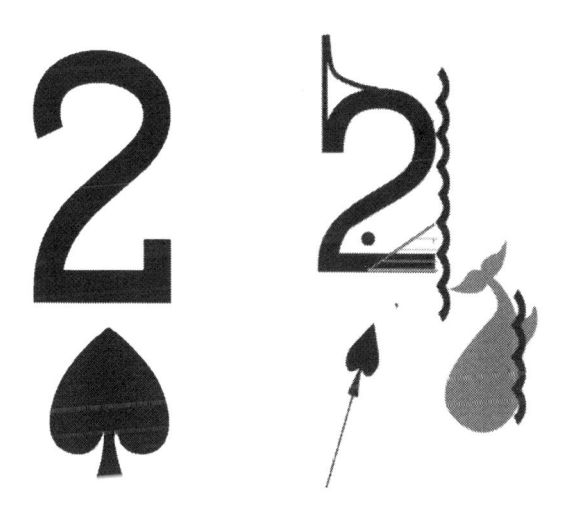

The Two of Spades looks like a whale threatened by a harpoon.

The Three of Spades looks like a pitch fork and a garden spade.

The Four of Spades looks like a flamingo over a lily pad.

WMTF™ Manual

The Five of Spades looks like a pizza cutter and the spade pulls the pizza from the oven.

The Six of Spades is a saxophone over a sheet music stand.

The Seven of Spades is a fishing pole and the spade looks like a fish.

The Eight of Spades looks like a guitar.

The Nine of Spades looks like an angry Venus fly trap.

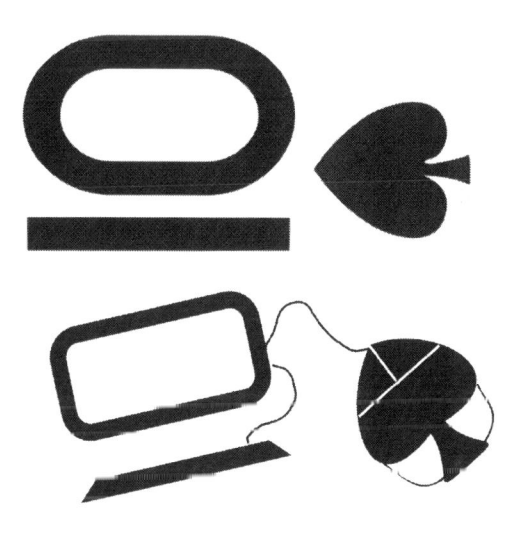

The Ten of Spades looks like a computer and the spade is the mouse.

The Jack of Spades looks like a black umbrella.

The Queen of Spades looks like a grave site.

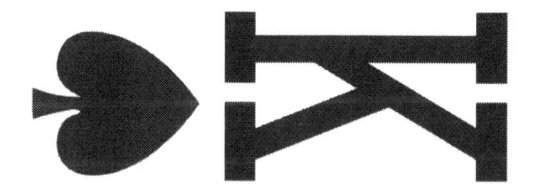

WMTF™ Manual

The King of Spades looks like a T-Rex chased by a spear.

Hearts

The Ace of Hearts looks like a tower with a balloon.

The Two of Hearts looks like a dagger.

The Three of Hearts looks like wavy hair and a comb.

The Four of Hearts looks like a sailboat.

The Five of Hearts looks like a unicycle on a stone road.

The Six of Hearts looks like a golf club over a tee.

The Seven of Hearts looks like the edge of a cliff with and buoy in the water below.

The Eight of Hearts looks like an ice-cream cone.

The Nine of Hearts looks like an axe about to split the heart.

shoots hearts.

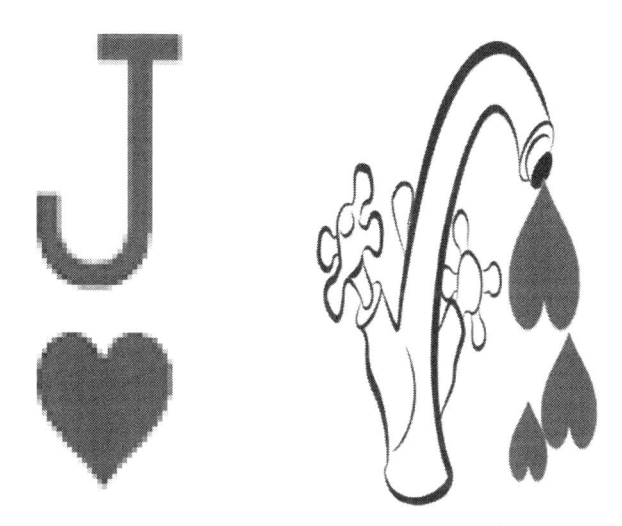

The Jack of Hearts looks like a water faucet pouring hearts out.

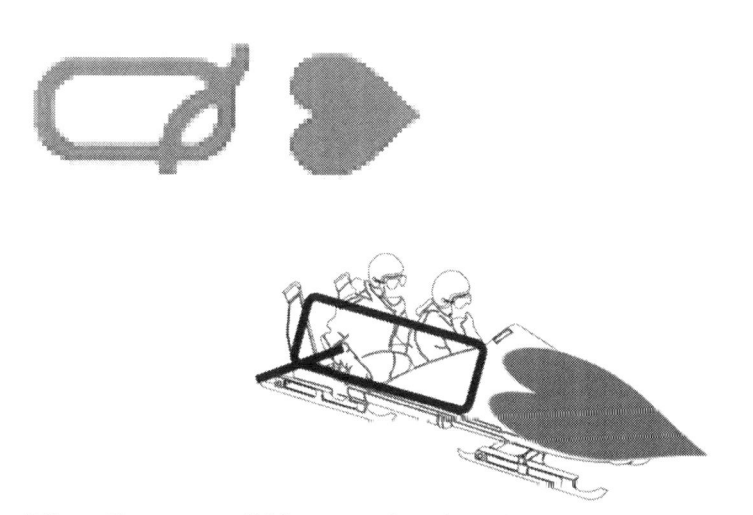

The Queen of Hearts looks like a bobsled team.

The King of Hearts looks like a pair of scissors cutting out a valentine.

WMTF™ Manual

Clubs

The Ace of Clubs looks like a green house with cover plants inside.

The Two of Clubs looks like a swan eating clovers.

The Three of Clubs looks like a fork to eat lettuce.

The Four of Clubs looks like wrapped presents.

The Five of Clubs looks like curling rocks lined up. If you don't know what that is, look it up.

The Six of Clubs looks like a speed boat where the club is the propeller.

The Seven of Clubs looks like a hockey stick with pucks. Can you tell I'm Canadian?

The Eight of Clubs looks like a vase of flowers.

WMTF™ Manual

The Nine of Clubs looks like a snail crawling to a clover.

The Ten of Clubs looks like an angry guy eating salad.

The Jack of Clubs looks like fish hook, full of weeds.

The Queen of Clubs looks like a tub with old style taps.

The King of Clubs looks like a ceiling fan with the "k" acting as a brace holding up the ceiling.

Diamonds

The Ace of Diamonds looks like a rocket and the diamond is the propulsion.

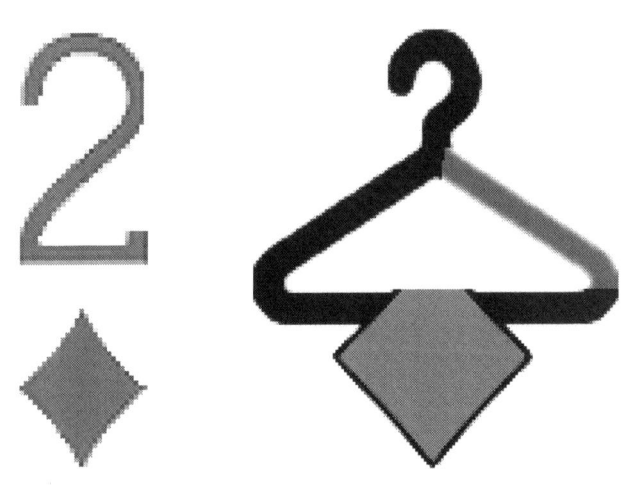

The Two of Diamonds looks like a clothes hanger with a cloth on it.

WMTF™ Manual

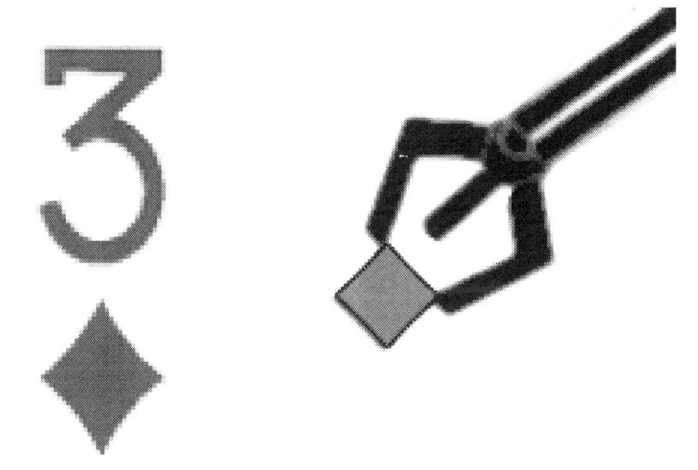

The Three of Diamonds looks like a robot arm claw.

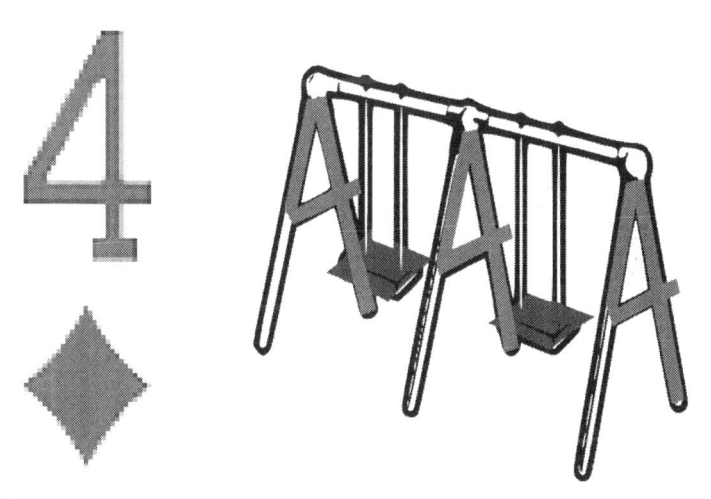

The Four of Diamonds looks like a swing and the diamond is the seat.

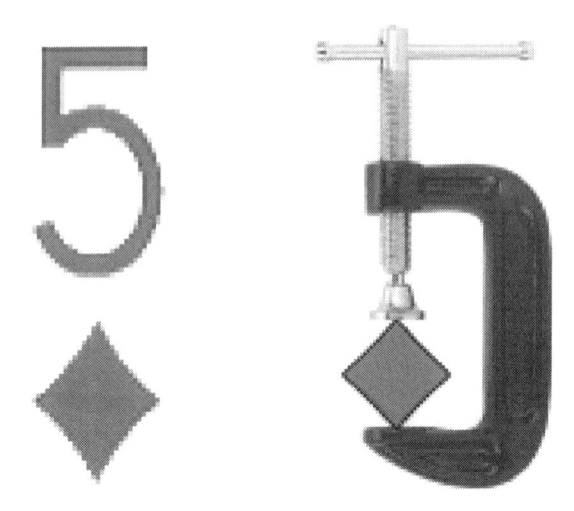

The Five of Diamonds looks like a workshop vice holding a diamond.

The Six of Diamonds looks like a paperclip and the paper is the diamond.

The Seven of Diamonds looks like a hammer hitting a diamond.

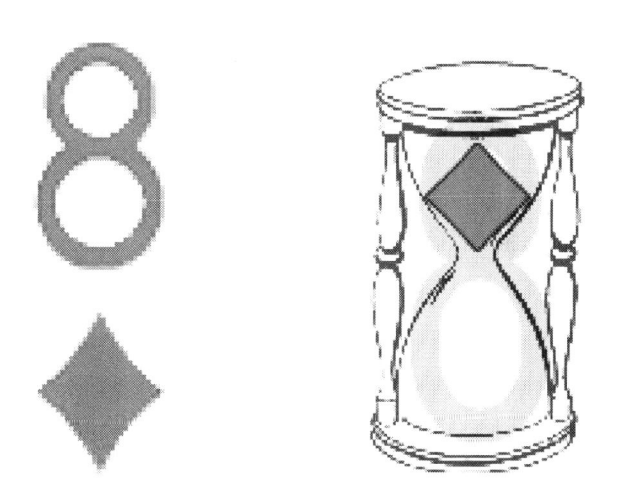

The Eight of Diamonds looks like a sand timer and the diamond is the sand.

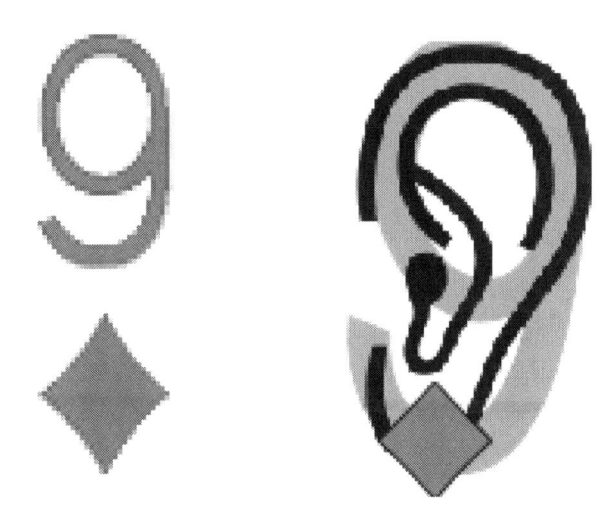

The Nine of Diamonds looks like an ear with a diamond earring on it.

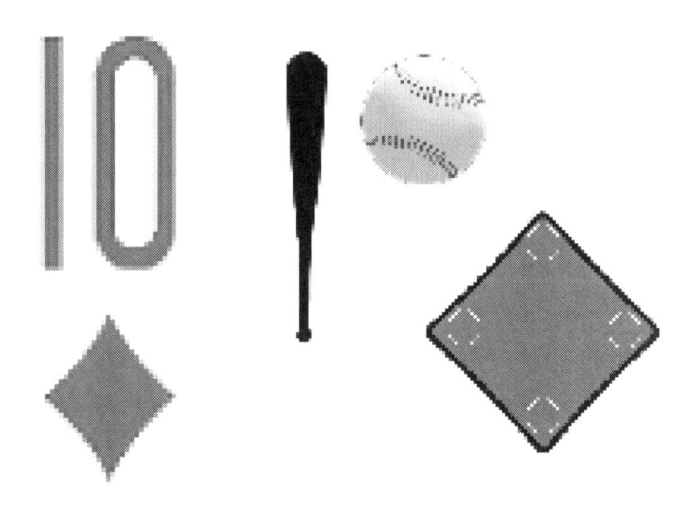

The Ten of Diamonds looks like a baseball bat and ball over a baseball diamond.

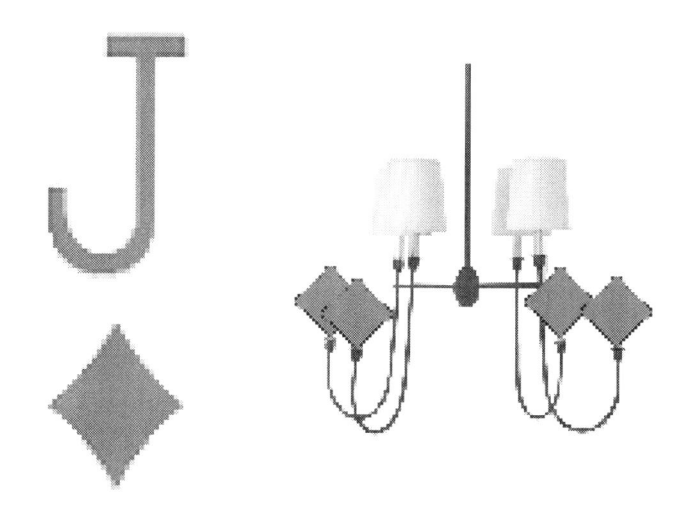

The Jack of Diamonds looks like a chandelier.

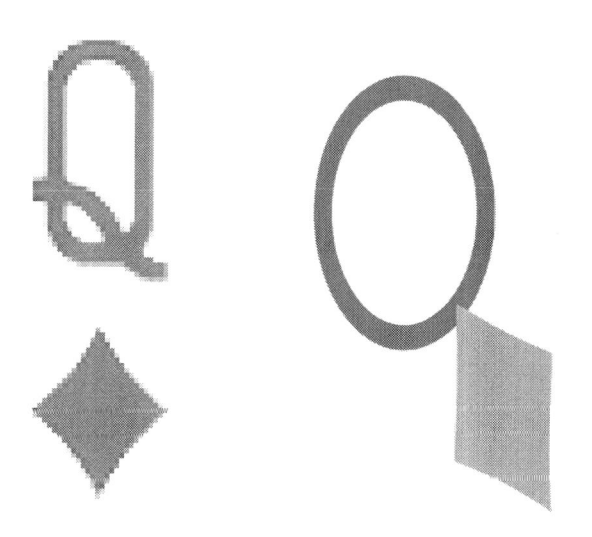

The Queen of Diamonds looks like a diamond ring.

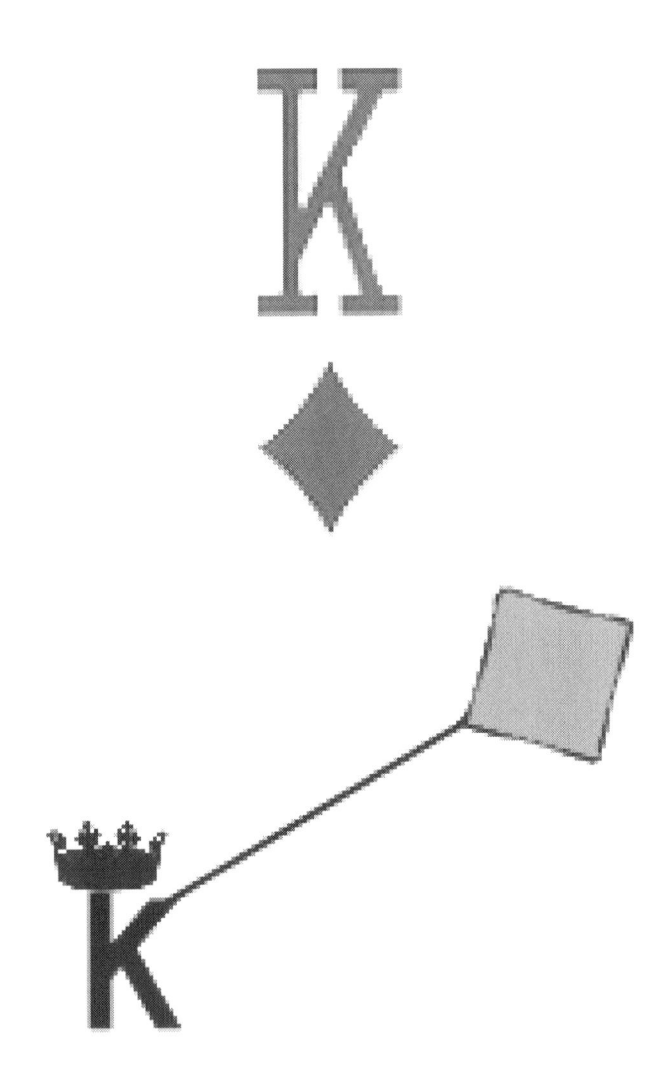

The King of Diamonds looks like a king flying a kite.

Flash Cards

Here's a good exercise to help master this list. Take a moment out and flip through a deck of cards. Use a pen and card by card, draw these pictures on one corner by the number and symbol, just like you saw in the pictures I provided.

You don't need to be perfect or a good artist but simply drawing out the peg on each card will help engrain it in your mind.

Use the deck as flash cards. Shuffle it and flip the cards down one at a time to test yourself and reinforce the links. The great thing about this method is that you only need to use one corner to make your flash cards. When you're ready you can turn the deck around and test your recall by looking at the blank end of the cards that you did not draw on. Take your practice deck around with you and memorize cards using the objects in the links.

Now that you know the **Farrow Method Card Technique**© you can amaze your friends and family by recalling cards from memory. This will also give you an advantage in card games.

The Linking Method

Remember the list of 20 objects from the first lesson? By now you probably have noticed they are also pegs for this card technique.

Here is the list of random objects you memorized and the cards they turn into:

1. Plane = Ace Spades
2. Ice Cream = 8 of Hearts
3. Whale = 2 Spades
4. Diamond Ring = Queen Diamonds
5. Computer = 10 Spades
6. Snail = 9 Clubs
7. Fishing Pole = 7 Spades
8. Clothes Hanger = 2 Diamonds
9. Umbrella = 2 Spades
10. Tower = Ace Hearts
11. Sailboat = 4 Hearts
12. Rocket = Ace Diamonds
13. Grave = Queen Spades
14. Robot = 3 Diamonds
15. Earrings = 9 Diamonds
16. Pitchfork = 3 Spades
17. Swan = 2 Clubs
18. Axe = 9 Hearts
19. Swinging Chair = 4 Diamonds
20. Bowl of Salad = 3 Clubs

See, you already know how to memorize cards!

The Elimination Technique

Before we end this chapter I'm going to add one more simple application of your new found card memory skills.

It's called the **Elimination Technique** and it will give you the ability to do a magic trick that no one will believe. It can also be used in many card games to predict which cards are left in the deck and which cards have already been played.

My favourite use of this technique is as a party trick. It's amazing to see it practiced and everyone will be amazed by your memory power.

The technique is simple. Use the **Farrow Method Card Technique©** found earlier in this chapter. Memorize it. This is not hard. After flipping through the deck a few times you will only get stuck on a few pegs. The peg list is visual so it is easier to recall than any other card list.

Next, get someone to shuffle a deck. You may want to use only half of a deck if you are a beginner at this technique or if you want the trick to go faster.

Get a volunteer, or two or three, to take a few cards from the deck. About four or five cards is a good number and makes for a really good effect.

Now, ask the volunteers take hide the chosen cards from you and give you the rest of the deck. They can shuffle it if they like to add to the magic.

You simply flip through the deck in your hands and view each card one at a time.

Every time you see a card, you must eliminate it with a simple visualization trick.

This elimination technique is actually easier than linking it because you don't need to connect two items that have no logical connection. You just need to mentally scratch it off your list so that you know which cards are still in the deck.

How Do We Do This?

Take the peg for the Four of Hearts, for example, which is a sailboat. To eliminate it, you must do something memorable to it like burn it, freeze it, or poke holes in it. Basically, damage it or change it radically in some way.

But What Is The Result?

At the end of the trick, flip through the peg list in your head. Go in order from Ace to King for each suit.

When you go back through the list of cards in your mind, the cards that you did not change or damage will stick out like a sore thumb in your mind's eye. Then you can rhyme off the missing cards from memory to the amazement of everyone.

Do this trick as often as you like, just remember to use a different elimination method each time to separate the decks in your head. For example, for the first deck you can poke holes in the cards and for the next deck and peg, set each card on fire, freeze it, and so on.

You can use this trick in bridge as well. Using the same example, if you see the Four of Hearts (Sailboat) you would imagine the boat burning on the water. And so on, as you see the cards being played.

Ask yourself whether a certain card has been played, then just look to the list in your head. If it has already been played, it will be eliminated; if not, it will stick out clearly.

Once again, in the next hand, you should pick a different action to eliminate the cards. If you burned the cards mentally in the last hand, then do something else to the peg like cover it in ice or split it in half. This way, you don't get it confused with the cards you eliminated from a previous hand or round.

Take a moment out right now and try this yourself.

Good Luck!

Chapter 7

How Do I Start a Memory Club?

Jack Smart: Part Two - Smarty Pants
Story by Dave Farrow

After Jack was diagnosed it felt like all the teachers talked differently to him, as if being diagnosed with ADHD and dyslexia suddenly made him half deaf and slow. It felt almost creepy to Jack. One teacher handed him some papers while explaining the exercise. The teacher kept nodding his head after each line like an instructional bobble head doll.

"Ok Jack, first you put your name here," (nod, nod)

"Then you answer the first three questions." (nod, nod and smile)

"Then you read this section." (nod, smile, nod)

It was so distracting that Jack asked him to repeat part of it, and then regretted asking. The teacher paused his non-verbal convulsive affirmations and gave him that look of smug knowing. His face said, "You're not as smart as me."

Jack was in math class.

"This can't get any worse." He thought. Then the bell rang.

His next class was with Mr. Muller, an English teacher. Mr. Muller was a firm teacher. He was tall, well over 6 feet and he had a full beard and wire-rimmed glasses. He spoke in an interesting way that was almost like a New York City accent but with a twist – as though his first language was German.

He made a point of holding his students to a high standard, so it wasn't an easy course, but he made it fun. He was the kind of teacher whom you wanted to impress. As a result he was one of the most loved teachers in the school.

Jack seemed to ooze into the room dragging his feet and looking at the floor. He poured his defeated frame in the chair.

"Sit up straight Jack. This isn't a soup kitchen." Mr. Muller barked at Jack. "Now stop staring off into space and open your book. Time to dive into the works of Billy Shakespeare."

This was Mr. Muller's usual playful tone so Jack perked up for a moment. He followed along with the class and half way through he was smiling and enjoying the lesson.

It took a while to sink in, but Jack finally realised that Mr. Muller was not talking down to him. Rather, he was treating Jack just as badly (or well) as he had in the past, before the diagnosis. Jack had never before enjoyed being told what to do so much.

But then lunch bell rang...

"Jack, can you stick around for a bit?" Mr. Muller asked. "Unless you have a peace treaty to negotiate or something?" he added sarcastically.

"No," Jack replied, not really understanding the teacher's sense of humour entirely, "I can stick around for a bit."

"I noticed you're really admiring your shoes today. Are they new?" Mr. Muller asked.

"No I'm not admiring my shoes." Jack replied, still not getting the humour.

"Well then, why is Jack Smart-aleck, my most disruptive, outgoing, and annoying student sitting quietly in the corner staring at the floor for the whole class?" he teased.

"Very funny." Jack answered.

"That still doesn't answer my question." Mr. Muller pressed. "What's the matter?"

"I thought all the teachers were told." Jack paused and took a deep breath. "I was diagnosed ADHD and Dyslexic last week."

"Ok, I knew about that. But what else?" Muller countered.

"What else? That's enough." Jack got angry. "It sucks, and I'm being treated differently." he vented. "It feels like everyone thinks I'm stupid."

"Who's doing this?" Mr. Muller asked, digging for more answers.

"Well they're not doing it on purpose I guess. It just feels like that. They just talk to me like I'm stupid. Like I'm slow."

"So what are you going to do about it?" Mr. Muller asked. "You can't keep staring at your shoes all day."
"Well I have a tutor and I'm working on my memory with memory techniques." Jack continued.

"What memory techniques?" Mr Muller asked, interested.

Jack explained about the World Memory Tournament Federation™ and how you could take a few simple lessons and do things like memorize strings of numbers and words. He explained that his mind seemed to come alive when he practiced the techniques, but he wasn't able to show the other teachers or students what he could do with his memory.

As Jack shared the memory skills he learned, Mr. Muller's eyes went wide. He was sceptical at first at the outrageous claims Jack made but once he demonstrated the list technique to him and recalled a random list of 20 objects from memory, Mr. Muller was convinced.

Next came numbers. Mr. Muller started writing a number on the board. He wrote out 25 digits and Jack went to work memorizing them.

Then he recalled them: 3141592… A few minutes later Jack had correctly recalled all of the numbers from memory with only two errors.

Mr. Muller's jaw dropped.

"I have been teaching for 30 years and I've never seen anything like that. Are you a natural genius?" Mr. Muller was awestruck.

Slowly the energy of the room shifted. The student had become a teacher, and Jacks confidence grew.

Jack started teaching him some of the secrets behind the techniques. He talked about the difference between sport memory and practical methods. Jack started with the sport and wanted more practice and wanted to start a memory club at the school but needed a teacher.

"I'll sponsor the club at the school." Mr Muller said. "I've heard of memory feats before but nothing as organized as this is. It's fascinating. I'd love to run it."

"That's awesome! Thanks!" Jack smiled. "The only problem is, how do we get people to join the club?"

"I think I have an idea that will solve both problems." Mr Muller smiled. "Have you ever read the book, *The Life of Pi*?"

"No" Jack answered.

"In the book, the main character is called a bad nick name and decides to do a memory feat to change how others look at him." Mr. Muller explained.

Jack's Slice of Pi

Math Class, Two Weeks Later:

Jack bounced in with a spring in his step and a smile on his face.

"You seem happy today Jack". The teacher nodded to the air as if agreeing with himself. Mr. Colbert was jack's math teacher.

Mr. Muller entered the room behind Jack and followed him into the room.
"Sorry for the interruption Benny, but this is the thing I told you about earlier. Jack is going to do that demonstration I told you about."

"All you said in the teachers' lounge was to block off part of today and a student will impress me," Mr Colbert, replied, "but I didn't think you were talking about Jack…"

"Why not? Jack's a smart kid… it's in his name after all." Mr. Muller mused, winking at Jack. He knew what was going to happen.

Mr. Colbert, or Benny as Mr. Muller called him took a breath and tried another approach.

"Mr. Muller, I respect you a lot, and I don't know what you're planning, but this is a math class here and we can't just do anything." Thinking a bit more he added "I just don't want Jack to be embarrassed. So what is this demonstration?"

"I am going to recall a thousand digits of Pi." Jack blurted out.

> **PI:** Pi is a transcendental number fundamental to mathematics. It is the ratio of the circumference to the diameter of any circle. It is commonly rounded to about 3.14159 but the decimal places of this number go on forever. It is used for many mathematical functions. It is also is the most well known random number and used by memory experts to demonstrate their abilities.

Mr. Colbert was speechless and sure he was being tricked.

"That's impossible! I mean, to recall 100 digits of PI would take weeks of effort."

"I spent a whole weekend on this so I'm ready!" Jack couldn't help but to brag, teasing the teacher a bit, enjoying the awkward moment.

The classroom laughed. A few students started talking amongst themselves making fun of Jack under their breath.

"It was Mr. Muller's idea. He read it in a book called *The Life of Pi*." Jack continued, enjoying the attention.

"Why don't we just get started," Mr. Muller suggested. "This will take some time after all."

Mr. Colbert tried to protest but couldn't think of anything to say. Pi was an iconic math number and they obviously had planned something important.

"I hope you know what you're doing." Mr. Colbert said to Mr. Muller as he invited Jack to the front of the room.

Jack fell into the teaching role very easily.

"Mr. Muller said this was the ultimate demonstration of memory. By doing this one demonstration, the main character in the book *The Life of Pi* was able to change how everyone saw him. It changed his life forever. He went from embarrassed to smart in one feat of memory."

"I am going to recall the nearly random sequence of numbers in the remainder of Pi to 1000 digits right now. Anyone can do things like this if you learn the secrets in our memory club." Jack continued.

Before anyone could say anything Jack walked to the front of the class and grabbed a piece of chalk. He started to write the digits of Pi on the board:

3.1415..9..2..6..5..3..5..8..9..7..9..3..2..3..8.4.6.. 2...6...4...3...3...8...3...2...7...9...5...0...........

Mr. Colbert rushed to take out a calculator and read the digits of PI to 10 and they were right but Jack was already past 25 digits.

"Come on man, you're the math teacher. You must have a book with Pi in it right?" Mr. Muller teased the math teacher. He believed in Jack and as an English teacher he enjoyed teasing a math teacher.

Ben Colbert walked to the back of the class and pulled out an old dusty math book that had Pi written in the inside cover as part of a decoration and started to check. To his surprise, every number Jack wrote was correct.

Jack was past 100 digits now and was running out of space on the board, even though he was writing smaller. It took 150 digits to get him to the side board. The class was amazed and looked around him for a cheat sheet or code written nearby but they found none.

As Jack passed 200 digits, the inside cover of the old book was not long enough and they had to refer to technology. Every student pulled out their smart phones and followed along. Because this was such a unique situation, nobody cared about the usual ban on smart phones in the classroom. Mr. Colbert was checking his tablet and an online listing of Pi to 1000 digits.

Jack was quickly running out of board space. By digit number 300, they had reached the end of the board without a mistake!

"Let's continue it in my class." Mr Muller said.

The entire math class, along with a few interested onlookers, followed Mr. Muller and Jack down the hall to Mr. Muller's class and Jack started filling the boards with numbers. Students had Pi up on their phones and were following along. The students were shouting out each number as Jack wrote it down. Before long, other classes heard the noise and when they discovered what was happening, they crowded into Mr. Muller's room to watch.

7..5..8..6..9..4.....

At 500 digits there was no more space on the board. The whole group moved on to the next classroom and Jack began filling another chalk board.

2..3..1..7..2..5..3..5..9..4..0......

At the 700th digit the principal walked into the class. They had moved to the big art class at the end of the hall because it could hold more people and had plenty of chalk board space.

Jack was using a step stool to reach the top of the board and make a better use of space.

The tension built as they reached 900 digits and counting. Jack felt the energy of the moment and it drove him to reach the finish line until finally...

1000 digits of Pi recalled from memory!

Jack paused to look at the board and realized he was breathing heavy from the excitement. He turned around and nearly the whole school clapped and cheered behind him.

He saw that every faculty member and nearly every student he knew had crammed into this one classroom to watch. The math teacher was the first to talk after the clapping died down.

"Jack, how did you do that?" he finally asked.
"Join my Memory Club and I'll show you. Anyone can do it with practice. I can teach you how." Jack explained.

Mr. Muller stepped in, "It's actually a mental sport from the World Memory Tournament Federation™. We're starting a club here at school for people interested in training in this skill and representing our school at regional and national competitions. I am sponsoring the club and Jack here is the head coach. So if you want to learn how to do cool things like this, just sign up for the club. We meet every Tuesday for 10 weeks."

Mr. Muller turned to Jack and winked and whispered "And that's how you start a memory club."

Chapter 8

Memory Tournament Rules?

Rules and Regulations – By Dave Farrow

Once you discover some basic memory techniques, it's fun to see how far you can go with it. With a little practice you will find that you can take the list technique and memorize hundreds or even thousands of items in a row. Then you can see how fast you can go.

That's how memory tournaments were born - as an honest attempt to push the brain to its limits and also have fun and show off while doing it and along the way arm students with the skills to succeed in academics!

The basic game is simple.

You Will Need:

Two Players

A Judge or Spectator

A Timer

A Monumentum™

The Monumentum™

A Monumentum™ is the official information that Memory Club Players memorize during the game. It sits in the middle of the table between tournament players.

The term Monumentum™ comes from a Latin word that means a recording for the purpose of remembrance. It is where we get the word monument.

Monuments are often huge structures that only serve the purpose to help us remember something important in the past like a battle or invention. It is the oldest form of memory technique. At the Memory Tournament Federation™ we see memory games as mental feat that is monumental.

Any information can be used as a Monumentum™ such as random numbers, foreign language vocabulary, technical terms and scripture, but only official Tournament Federation Monumentum™ forms will be allowed for competition and ranking.

Monumentums™ are found in your club kit or online at: **www.memorytournament.com**

For a proper memory tournament game there are two phases: the **Pre-Match Memorizing Round** and the **Recall Match**.

Pre-Match Memorizing Round

1. Find a partner who wants to play this game. You can also use our computer opponent in our web based Tournament Trainer or our mobile Tournament Trainer App. Check our website often for new practice games and training options.

2. If the other player does not know memory techniques yet, have them learn the list technique by reading the lesson in this book or watching the video on our website.

3. Use a **Monumentum**™ to memorize. You can find **Practice Level** and **Tournament Ranked Monumentums**™ on our website as well as in the memory club kit.

4. Place the Monumentum™ between the two players, but don't peak at the content. Neither player should have prior knowledge of the Monumentum™ contents. Make sure you order fresh pages from **www.memorytournament.com** before an official club game so all scores are valid.

5. The Judge should set the timer and confirm that both players are ready.

6. The judge signals the game to begin and starts the timer, and flips over the Monumentum™ so both players can see it. This begins the **Memorizing Round**.

7. The players use all the skills they have trained for to memorize the information!

8. When the timer stops OR both players agree to stop memorizing, the round is over. The judge should place the Monumentum™ at the edge of the table facing away from both players so neither player can see the contents. The judge should be the only person who can see the information. Get ready for players to face off in a **Recall Match**.

That was the **Memorizing Round**. The real challenge is recalling the information perfectly during the **Recall Match**.

Recall Match: Step by Step

1. Flip a coin or use rock, paper, scissors to determine the starting player. The person who wins the toss does not automatically go first. Whoever wins the coin toss has the **option** to either start first or pass to the other player. This choice will be determined by the strategy the player uses.

2. Player #1 will state the first item in the **Monumentum**™ list.

3. Player #2 will counter by saying the second item in the list and the game is on. Back and forth, the players say the next item in the list until one player makes a mistake.

4. When a mistake is made the judge should stop the match, declare that a mistake was made, and call out the real answer. The first mistake signals a stop to the **Recall Match**.

5. Before a winner is announced, the player who did not make the mistake needs to recall at least one more item in the list, to prove that they actually remembered more than the opponent. If they can't recall the next item then the match is a draw. This is called the **One to Win Rule**™.

6. If the match is not a draw, the player with no mistakes is declared the winner of the match.

7. Repeat and have fun.

One-to-Win Rule™:

After playing the memory tournament game for a while it was discovered that ending the game after one person makes a mistake was unfair. After all, the losing player had recalled just as many items as the winner. That sounds more like a tie than a win.

Basically, if you're playing a memory tournament game and your opponent makes a mistake, you still have to prove you memorized more items than they did, in order to say you won.

So in the interest of fairness all tournament games adopted the One-To-Win Rule™.

When Player #1 makes a mistake on say the 36th number the judge should stop the match and declare that a mistake was made and call out the real answer. At this point, the match is considered a draw.

The judge then asks the opponent who did not make the mistake to recall the next item in the sequence. If they recall correctly then they are declared the winner.

Without this rule, novice players could theoretically win a match without recalling anything.

For the record, there is one other way a draw could be declared. If both players go all the way down the Monumentum™ and recall of the information planned for that match, and there is no information left to recall, then it would also be a draw.

For final tournament games that end in a draw, the match will be repeated until there is a winner.

The Bragging Rule:

After one player makes a mistake, the opponent can recall the next item and is encouraged to recall as many of the items left in the sequence as possible. This number will be recorded but does not affect the rank, as they have already won. This allows the winning player to show how far they could have gone and showcases their great memory to intimidate future challengers.

Basically, after one player loses, the other gets to brag and show off. Are you a memory master that can show off? Or do you need to practice your skill more?

The Recording Rule:

To qualify in official WMTF™ ranking, all matches must be recorded. A simple hand held device or phone is all that's necessary. These videos will be posted online on the official tournament channel so other players can see the match. Please see the website for tutorials on how to post videos.

The Winner:

All players will agree to a set of rules before starting a match. When the match is over, the Judge declares a winner and the players shake hands in the spirit of good sportsmanship.

In a larger tournament with numerous players, choosing a single winner becomes more complex, so make sure to familiarize yourself with official WMTF™ Tournament Rules.

Official Rule Variants

For new and experienced players the following variations will ensure that this game is always inclusive, challenging and exciting.

Time Limit Variant:

Each player gets a reasonable time to recall their **Monumentum**™ data during the **Recall Match**. To keep the game going at a reasonable pace the judge may use a timer to prompt quicker answers from a player if it looks like they have forgotten anything, or are taking too long to respond.

For example, Player #1 calls out the first item on the list but Player #2 doesn't answer right away is struggling to remember. The judge can then prompt Player #2 by asking if they need more time. If the player is unresponsive or taking excessive time to recall their item from the list, the judge can give a deadline: "You have 10 more seconds to answer." If the player answers correctly, the game continues. If the player answers incorrectly, the game is over. If the player still does not call out an answer, it is treated the same as an incorrect answer. If you follow this rule then no answer is the same as the wrong answer.

Players and judges should agree ahead of time on the time limit. This should be at least 10 seconds, but no more than 60 seconds, just to keep a quick game pace.

Note: When using the time limit rule DO NOT allow the judge and/or spectators to count down out loud. This would be a distraction that is unfair to the players. Save the out loud count downs for New Year's Eve!

For some ranked tournaments players will use a two clock timer, often used in chess matches, to ensure they don't take too long to recall. Just like in chess matches, each time a player recalls an item they hit the plunger, then the timer waits for the opponent to do the same.

1 Minute Memory:

In this variation players are given only One Minute to memorize as much of the Monumentum™ as possible during the pre-match Memorization Round. Also, during the Recall Match, players have only 5 seconds to recall their item and say an answer, before their time is up. If a player does not recall the item correctly within 5 seconds then the match is over.

Judges should use a stop watch or a two clock timer to ensure unbiased tracking of time.

Infinite Game Variant:

In this variation the players get an unlimited time to recall their item. This variation is great for new players who are not as practiced at memory, to ease the pressure of recalling quickly.

Three Strikes Variant:

As the name implies, the match keeps going until one person has made over 3 mistakes instead of just one.

Distraction Variant:

The goal of this variation is for players to get used to dealing with distractions while recalling information. Often used to train for a tournament, players can chose to add distractions to their game.

The best distraction for training is spoken word like talk radio or TV on in the background. When there is a conversation going on in the background when a player is trying to recall, it raises the difficulty level for memorization and recall.

In addition to TV and Radio on in the background, other distractions can include: doing the match in a moving vehicle like a bus or car, doing the match in a crowded cafeteria, or in bleachers or seats where an athletic sport is being played or practiced.

The main idea is that other sensory stimulation is involved in a limited background capacity. This helps players learn to concentrate so they will be better able to compete later, during tournaments.

Warning!

DO NOT play a match while your teacher is speaking to the class or teaching a lesson. When the teacher catches you ignoring the classroom lesson, you will most likely get a detention!

If playing in a bus or car, **NEVER** distract the driver.

If you are old enough to drive, **DO NOT** play a match while you are driving a vehicle. Please focus on the rules of the road and stay safe while driving.

Psyche Out Variant:

Practice this Variant because it will be used during major tournaments from time to time to make the game more exciting to watch!

This is an exciting variation and even more extreme than the **Distraction Variation**. The goal is to "psyche out" the other player and make them lose focus.

When one player is recalling an item the opponent is allowed to distract the Recaller verbally and visually in any way they wish, without touching them. Both players must agree to this rule before the game begins.

Common distraction tactics include: waving your arms in the air as a visual distraction and yelling random numbers or cards out loud to trick opponent into saying the wrong item. This raises the difficulty of memory feats considerably and can be exciting and entertaining to watch, so get creative with your distractions.

Warning!

This tactic can backfire. Don't be so focused on tricking your opponent that you lose your place in the data set being recalled. If you focus too much on the psyche out, you risk making a mistake yourself.

Vocabulary Variant:

Changing the information on the **Monumentum**™ can add fun and real life memory skills to the game. Improving your vocabulary is one thing that helps influence how people judge you in life. A better vocabulary also makes you smarter.

Try using foreign language information or higher level vocabulary words in a game. Make sure the vocabulary words are random and that no one playing has experience with that language. This can be a great game for foreign language classes and even to expand English courses.

Learning vocabulary is a big part of learning a language and mastering the spoken word. Using memory techniques is by far the fastest way to acquire native and foreign language vocabulary.

Teachers:

Try getting students to compete for prizes based on how many words they recall. Visit the website **www.memorytournament.com** for lesson plans, programs on learning vocabulary and additional Monumentums™ with randomized language vocabulary.

All Stressed Variant:

Combine the **One Minute Memory** variation AND the **Psyche Out Rule** for a high intensity winner-takes-all sudden death match!

Chapter 9

Tournament Security and Structure

WORLD MEMORY TOURNAMENT FEDERATION

Official Security Standards

The reason matches need to be recorded is to uphold a clear standard of credibility, so we only use the strictest guidelines. WMTF™ security guidelines are adopted from the world's most trusted source for memory records – the Guinness Book of Records.

In the past, some memory competitions have had inconsistent standards. Things like friends of players acting as judges and changing scores to scoring mistakes that lead to re-counts and even title changes have been common.

The Guinness Book of Records solved this problem early by using technology. Every important memory record is recorded and witnessed from start to finish. For every record to be broken there must be an official Guinness Record judge present OR the record must be painstakingly documented, with credible witnesses AND a certain amount of film and print media.

Most record breakers today can't afford to fly out a judge and pay for their accommodations so they follow the guidelines for submitting record breaking attempts to Guinness. There are many requirements for these submissions but video evidence is strongly recommended and in most cases, even required, along with official application forms. Things like TV News coverage and continuous video recording of event from multiple cameras make for a strong record breaking attempt and eliminate any grounds for error or accusation.

Cameras often see things that people miss, especially if the match is very exciting. Recording the match serves as a precaution and will prevent any suggestion of cheating. The tournament style also ensures that scoring is done during the match, not in another room afterwards, which only increases the security and credibility of the game. All matches will be submitted with the serial number for the Monumentum™ used so past matches can be easily verified at any time.

By using these guidelines, the WMTF™ makes every effort to ensure that every tournament in the world is held to the same standard. No matter who you are or where you live, just one hand-held camera and video footage of your tournament is all you need to participate in the official ranking system. You don't need to pay for a large space and specially trained judges. With modern technology and growing accessibility around the world, it doesn't take much to start competing. Please visit the website for how to properly film a match.

Other Memory Ranks and Accomplishments:

The WMTF™ recognizes that other memory accomplishments exist outside of our own organization and may include titles and ranks too. In the spirit of good sportsmanship, the WMTF™ keeps friendly relationships with all memory master as well as other memory trainers and experts.

The WMTF™ welcomes competitors from everywhere because we know that players in our league will go try other feats too. Memory masters from all over are encouraged to try our new tournaments and seasoned experts may find that the tournament style is a fresh new alternative. Memory veterans will definitely meet new competitors to teach, mentor or compete against.

Also, we realize that memory competitions in general will never have a large following unless the governing bodies or organizations are credible. Therefore all matches that receive any ranking at all need to be recorded. All Grand Mastership and Senoki™ level challenges will need to be filmed and posted. No tournament game will be considered official unless properly filmed using randomly generated verified material.

Every time I Broke a Guinness Record I had to follow a specific set of rules for filming every bit of memorizing and recalling. It takes extra time but it's worth it. I had a few critics who tried to say my record was done improperly but no one took them seriously because the strict rules followed by the Guinness Book of Records.

The same is true for the World Memory Tournament Federation™.

We may chose to recognize titles and feats of memory from past events and performances however they will not all be considered valid until we have footage of the event on record.

These titles and ranks fall into 2 categories – **Verified** and **Unverified**. If you can prove your rank to our level of security standards then we can verify it and transfer the ranking to our league. If not, then the title is considered unverified as per WMTF™ rules and we may list it on our website but do not attest to its validity.

We can still give kudos nonetheless. In case of unverified titles or champs, they can definitely start from scratch in our league to get verified here too, and add this WMTF™ title to their list of accomplishments OR **re-perform** their other memory feat on camera with our protocols

We will also be highlighting memory feats performed before competitions existed. Like when Harry Lorayne recalled the studio audience on The Tonight Show in the 1980's. Other mentalists and enthusiasts have performed similar note worthy feats of memory.

If you have a title that you want recognized please contact us for guidelines and we will help you get verified.

Tournament Structure:

Individual matches are always fun, but using your memory only gets more exciting when you have a full memory tournament. In a tournament, there are multiple rounds of matches and even different competition categories.

Every official WMTF™ tournament must be registered online in advance of the event date to get specific tournament level Monumentums™ and must adhere to WMTF™ Rules.

Because we provide many fun and optional rule variations, the preferred rules may vary from club to club and region to region. All rule variations are valid for both practice matches and full tournaments so clubs should agree in advance on which set of rules will be used.

Individual players can check the website for a list of tournaments in their local region or around the world. If there are no tournaments in your local area then contact your Regional Coordinator or the website.

WMTF™ Regional Coordinators are always available to help with your tournament needs. A Regional Coordinator is the official liaison to the WMTF™ and ensures that rules are followed during tournaments. Coordinators also help to start new clubs and connect players to clubs and tournaments. If there are no Regional Coordinators listed in your area, don't worry!

Contact us to learn how you can become a new Regional Coordinator OR to learn how another Coordinator can help run an event remotely.

Three Categories:

Official WMTF™ tournaments are divided into three categories for competition: **Words, Numbers and Cards**. Individual players have the option to compete in any one or two of the three categories, or all three.

For example, one player may only know the words technique and compete in just that category. There are already several elementary school clubs that focus only on the words category. They even use Monumentums™ that have words at their reading level.

Another player may have learned the numbers technique and want to compete in 2 categories, and another player still may want to compete in all 3 categories, for a full mental workout. All are welcome to compete.

Within each category, winners will be recognized for 1st place, 2nd place, 3rd place and 4th place ranking. Top scoring winners from each category (words, numbers, cards) will move on to compete in the finals. This final round will determine the overall tournament winner(s).

Before the tournament begins, all players must be registered so tournament organizers will have a complete list of players for each category. All players will use the same set of rules, agreed upon in advance by the Tournament organizers. This ensures that you know exactly which rules and variants will be used in the tournament and helps a player to practice and strategize.

Semi-Final Stage:

Within each tournament category, organizers will review the list of players and randomly select competing pairs, before the tournament starts. Players will compete until a winner is chosen. Winners are randomly paired off again, with other winners for another round of individual matches. Continue with this format where winners move up to the next level until there are only 8 players remaining. These 8 are the Semi Finalists, who will go on to play until only 4 final players are left. This is called the Final Four.

Final Four:

The Final Four players will again pair off and compete to determine the top two.

The 2 losing players of that match will compete in one final match for 3rd place and 4th place. The 2 winning players of the Final Four match will compete for 1st place and 2nd place. 1st, 2nd, 3rd, and 4th place winners are awarded winning ranks within their category and these Final Four will also move on to the final overall round.

Repeat this process for each category of competition until you have four winners in each category.
In both smaller and larger clubs, you may also find that a few of the same people are winners in more than just one category. This is normal. Because of this overlap the finals may not have 12 competitors (four per category) but only 4 in the finals or less in smaller clubs.

The overall final matches can be done with any even number of players.

In some cases, with smaller clubs and fewer players, there may only be 5-10 players total. In these cases it will take fewer matches and less time to complete a full tournament but the same basic structure is followed. Pair off and eliminate players until you get a Final Four, who will compete for the final title.

Drawing player names from a hat is a great way to choose which players are paired off for individual matches. Keep that hat close by, as it may come in handy later on!

Odd Numbers of Players:

In cases where there are an odd number of players for any round of competition, organizers should use **The Lottery Rule** to select paired opponents.

The Lottery Rule:

Because tournament competition is based on pairs of players competing head to head, having an odd number of players is a common problem, but an easy one to solve.

In any round, it's possible to have an odd number of players. For example, you could have 5 players in the Semi Final round because you started with 10 players.

In this case you need one more player to round out the game.

Take the names of the people eliminated in the last round and put them in a hat. This is the **Lottery Pool**. Draw one name at random. This one lucky person has just "won the lottery" and gets a pass to the next round, to even out the numbers.

Normally, when a player loses a match they are eliminated forever, but **The Lottery Rule** gives one **Lottery Winner** the chance to play again, win, and move to the next round.

If You Start With An Odd Number:

If the tournament is just starting and there are no previous Lottery Pool players to draw from, the lottery can still be applied. Begin the first round of matches for all other players while the odd-numbered player sits out. When the first round of matches is over, there is now a Lottery Pool of players from which to draw. Put these names in a hat and draw one lucky Lottery Winner. This lucky winner will play the odd-numbered player who sat out. Continue the tournament as usual.

Remember that the Lottery Pool consists only of players eliminated in the direct previous round.

Example: Larger Groups

Imagine that there are 23 players registered to compete in the word category. Players are paired off for individual matches – 11 pairs of 2 - for the first round. The odd-numbered 23rd player will sit out.

When the matches are done, there are 11 winners and 11 Lottery Pool players. Draw one name from the Lottery Pool who will pair off the 23rd player who sat out of the first round. Of these 2 players, one will be eliminated and the other will advance to the next round.

There are now 12 winners. Players are again randomly paired off for the next round of matches – this makes 6 pairs of 2. Finish matches to determine 6 new winners.

There are now 6 winners. Randomly pair off players into 3 pairs of 2 and begin matches.

There are now 3 winners. Remember that there must be 4 finalists for each category.

Use the Lottery Pool and choose one more Lottery Winner from the previous round – these players are Semi-Finalists.

Pair off the last 4 players into 2 pairs of 2. The final 2 winners will compete again for 1st place and 2nd place. Similarly, the final 2 losers will compete again for 3rd place and 4th place.

All 4 players should advance to the overall tournament final round. Yes that's right, the lottery may get a lucky person into the final round. Everyone loves an underdog.

Example: Smaller Groups

Many clubs that are just starting will have fewer members and players. This is common, but doesn't prevent the club from competing in official tournaments for official ranking and status.

Let's say there are 5 club members who want to host and compete in an official tournament.

The tournament starts with 4 players paired off – 2 pairs of 2 players – while the 5th player sits out.

After the first matches there are 2 winners and 2 losers. One of the 2 Lottery Pool players is selected to pair off with the 5th player and these two play another match. This leaves 3 winners in the first round and still 2 players in the Lottery Pool.

Two of the 3 winners pair off. A 4th player is drawn again from the Lottery Pool and the 4 Finalists square off as usual to determine rank and title, before advancing to the next category or final overall matches.

Small clubs like this can still compete with as few as 3 players. Player A and Player B compete. If Player B wins, then Player A competes with Player C. The loser of the Player A vs Player C match will take 3rd place and the winner will face Player B, to determine 1st and 2nd place. All three players will have official ranking in each category.

Forfeit Rule:

A player may choose at any time to drop out or forfeit their position in the tournament. This can happen if the player gets sick or just wants to stop.

Within each category (word, number, card), and before the Final Four winners are chosen, a player can forfeit their position at any time. At this point, a player who forfeits simply loses the opportunity to compete and advance. If a player drops out and there is an even number of players remaining, then continue the tournament. If a player drops out and there are an odd number of players remaining, use the Lottery Rule to continue the tournament.

If a player reaches the Final Four in any category (word, number, card) and wins 1st, 2nd, 3rd or 4th, he or she is unlikely to forfeit but is still allowed to forfeit or drop out. In this case, the player will keep their rank and title but lose the chance to compete in the overall tournament matches.

The remaining 3 Finalists will advance to the final overall tournament matches. This usually only happens if a finalist in one category has not trained in either of the other 2 categories.

> "The beauty of the memory tournament game is that it cannot be won, it can only be lost."
>
> Dave Farrow

Made in the USA
Lexington, KY
20 June 2015